# How We Listen Now:

## Essays and Conversations About Music and Technology

## By Cortney Harding

# Foreword

Ever since mid-1999, when Napster became the go-to source for young music fans, the recorded music industry has been struggling with how to adapt to the societal shift that had occurred. Musicians of all stripes were quick to condemn the technology that in their eyes was built to destroy their careers.

It has been almost eighteen years.

Cortney Harding is a deep thinker and cultural commentator who, during the last ten years spent four of them working for Billboard magazine. It was there that she realized that she had the music business background and the skills to help others navigate what she calls "…the treacherous waters of the music business." After leaving Billboard she began consulting with startups and writing articles and essays about the problems of the day facing the recorded music business and musicians.

Her approach to writing about today's music and technology world arrives with a martini-dry precision. For simply persevering in covering this troubled, maze-like space – those "treacherous waters" long ago swept the anti-technology crowd out to sea – Harding should receive your total admiration, as I know only too well what a tough beat it is.

By writing in clear and unaffected prose, she remains focused and delivers her critiques without snark; that lack of snark is very rare these days. At times, when reading her essays, one senses that she is trying to pick a fight with the reader. That is not her intention but it does keep the reader mindful of the insights she is sharing with you.

In conversation Harding is quick to accept that at times she has missed the mark in her predictions. Those honest admissions show the depth of her thinking and prove that she's not merely dumping out essays riddled with click-bait to get attention.

If this is the first time you have come across Harding's work, then this collection provides a very useful primer for what I'm sure will be her long career in leading the conversation around the expanding world of music and technology.

After all, it may have been eighteen years but there's still a long way to go.

Dave Allen

## Introduction

There's a classic Louis CK bit, "Everything's Amazing and Nobody's Happy," where he bemoans the fact that people take pretty much everything for granted. I'll fully admit that I'm a prime example of this – I've bitched about wi-fi speeds on every continent while ignoring the fact that I have the privilege to see the world. Seriously, don't ever travel with me to a place where the wi-fi is even a little suspect, because you'll wind up hating me.

I'm old enough to remember dial-up internet yet whine when my movie doesn't load instantly. I had flip phones for years and yet complain about my iPhone, which basically connects me to the sum of human knowledge in the palm of my hand. If you'd told me about Spotify – a place where I can listen to any song or album, in full, whenever I want to, for ten bucks a month – ten years ago, I would have thought it was the single greatest thing ever. Now, I write articles picking it apart, because it could have better social functions.

Let's face it – the present is boring. It's familiar, and familiarity breeds contempt. It's why we're jerks to the people we love, even though we value them, because we see them all the time. It's the reason people who grew up poor and got rich act like jerks to the help, because all they see is the reality that's in front of them at that very moment. Tina Fey has a funny bit about a homeless person at a fashion shoot who eventually starts asking for different catering and designers, because they accept the new normal that quickly.

So sure, I could try to do those things Oprah tells us to do – live in the moment! Exist with purpose and gratitude! Remember how hard it was to make plans before texting, or order food before Seamless, or creep on random people's vacation shots before Instagram! But nah, I'll just write about the future of music instead.

I started writing about music in high school, but didn't start writing about the music business until I started working at *Billboard* in 2007. The more time I spent there, the more I became fascinated with the intersection of music and technology, and how the old business was caught so utterly off-guard when Napster happened and things continued to melt down. I'm still shocked by the people who tilt at windmills and try to fight the future – do you sincerely, honestly believe that people will go back to buying CDs? What world do you live in?

The world I want to live in allows for artists from every corner of the globe to share their music and have a shot at being the next big thing, even if they don't know a guy who knows a guy. It allows for people to share content while also respecting copyright, but realizes that you gotta make money other ways if you want to be an artist. It allows for people to be creative in how they distribute and monetize their content and personalities.

The future is wide open and totally unsettled, and that's why I love writing about it. Who knows if messaging apps will replace streaming services, or apps will cease to be a thing, or if a service will go bust? I certainly don't, but it's fun as hell to ask the questions.

## 2014: The Year Nothing Broke, and Nothing Got Fixed

This was the year of the treadmill.

I mean that both for me personally (ever train for an ultra-marathon during a polar vortex?) and for the music business as a whole. 2014 felt like a whole lot of running, but there was no real forward movement – everyone wound up in pretty much the same place they started.

There were some big stories, of course. Beats Music launched, attracted something like 100,000 users, and then was snapped up by Apple for a cool $3 billion for...some reason, yet to be announced. Apple wants a streaming service, even though streaming services bleed money. Apple wants to be cool, because I know when I walk into a Bushwick coffeeshop, it's Dells as far as the eye can see. Apple wants to bundle the product with headphones, because selling a subpar product based on cool branding is the path to long term growth. Look, I'm sure they are going to do something amazing and I'll be forced to eat my words. But from where I sit, I'm still not seeing the logic.

Amazon Prime launched a streaming music service and no one seemed to care. YouTube finally launched their streaming service and no one seemed to care, although to be fair it's early and no numbers have been released. Deezer launched...something in the US and no one seemed to...you get the picture.

Spotify continued to grow, despite Taylor Swift's best efforts. They seem to be fairly comfortable with their lead, given that the last time I looked, they were hiring a full time staff member to throw parties for other staff members. Wonder how things will look when they sit down to renegotiate contracts with the labels?

A bunch of small startups launched; a bunch of small startups died. Circle of life and venture capital.

Because here's the real reason we're still on the treadmill – fundamentally, nothing has changed. Artists still write "songs," which are generally a few minutes long; they record and collect those songs on albums, which are released to the public on a pre-determined date. They do lots of press around those releases, and then they go on tour. Then they tour again, and again. Maybe they sell a song to a TV show, or an ad. Maybe a bunch of people at a music/tech conference have a panel called "Islands in the Stream" or "Radio on the TV" and talk about how this isn't "selling out" anymore. And the beat goes on, and on…

No one is asking the bigger question, which is "why albums?" Why are release dates? Hell, why any of this?

I understand artists and labels and radio need organizing principles. And I understand that this model has worked for a very long time. But it's worth considering that maybe it needs to shift a bit. Maybe artists should release content when it's ready, not when it's some pre-selected Tuesday. The technology exists for them to be recording all the time, wherever they are. Some artists, and I won't name names, are also recording whole album's worth of content that never sees the light of day – talk about a sunk cost. Unless it's absolute garbage, what's the harm in putting it out? Someone will probably like it.

The kids, as they say, have ever shorter attention spans. I'm not here to rag on millennials for their crippling ADHD – but I am here to say that they have millions more options than most of us ever had. Tinder is perfect site for them – infinite choices, and if you don't like something, move to the next thing and forget it. But they also have short memories, and if you serve them something different the next time and they like it, all is forgiven.

So clinging to this old model of releasing bodies of work on a given date, based on all that we know, seems a little off, doesn't it? And yes, right now some of you will want to Swift-boat me, but Tay-Tay is the exception, not the rule. She's the 1% of artists if ever there was one.

If I had a wish for 2015, it would be this: kill the album. For some artists, who really want to present a body of work and tell a story, fine, keep it. For everyone else, just scrap it. Albums probably started as a cynical ploy to get more money ("they only want one song, but they have to pay for twelve of them, even if eleven of them suck! Brilliant!") and this definitely reached a fever pitch in the nineties – and I should know, because I bought a lot of those albums. It became all filler, no killer, and then Napster laid waste to it.

So just start putting stuff out there. Kids are fine with imperfections. Some of the stuff they love on YouTube makes me feel seasick watching it because the camera work is so bad, but it doesn't matter. Release little clips of tracks and see what the response is. If it doesn't get a bite, toss some more chum in the water.

2014 was pretty much a wash, and that's OK. We're reaching the end of an era, and we've been reaching it for a long time now. A while ago, there was a political cartoon that had an illustration of every president since Kennedy saying one word, and it added up to "Don't worry, Castro will fall any minute now." It feels like you could replicate that with every editor of Billboard saying, "Don't worry, the old music biz model will fall any minute now." Rome wasn't built in a day, and it didn't collapse in one, either. But we don't want to get to the point of collapse – it's far better to pivot early and get ahead of the game.

# 2015: Will Buzzfeed Be The New Model for the Music Biz?

A note on my predictions: I am often wrong. On the podcast last year, I had about a .500 average, which makes me better than almost all the NYC-area professional sports teams, at least. I was right(ish) about music royalty payments becoming more mainstream news, if only because Taylor Swift made it an issue. I was right that streaming services would fail to crack the mainstream in the US, although they have grown (and are certainly mainstream in the Nordics). I was wrong about EDM continuing to dominate the charts (thank god!). I was wrong about Pandora continuing to piss off artists, which is good in the long run. And I was in the middle on viral videos – now everyone is doing them, so while they are driving traffic, the traffic might be more diluted than it once was.

But you should keep reading this, because I am right some of the time, and you can make fun of me if not. I'll be writing about one prediction today and another next week, so come back and see how I spent my holiday.

Anyway, back to the question posed above – will Buzzfeed become a model for the music business? That the site is wildly successful and influential is pretty much undisputed at this point. I've started hearing Buzzfeed correspondents on NPR shows, and much of their news coverage is excellent by any standard. The New York Times just laid off their labor reporter, and a few days later, Buzzfeed announced they were hiring a labor reporter. Doesn't take a weatherman to see which direction this particular wind is blowing.

But the great thing about Buzzfeed is that for every great piece for reporting on serious issues, they put out ten listicles of cats who are psyched that it's almost Christmas, or quizzes about which Gilmore Girl you are. Although they've hired seemingly every media person in the greater NYC and LA metro areas, Buzzfeed relies on its huge user community for much of its content – and therein lies the first lesson it can teach the music biz.

Major labels have a huge platform, and yet only a small handful of artists get to use it. When the cost of distribution was high, this made sense – you could only afford to print and ship so many CDs. But now that the cost of distribution is virtually nothing, opening up the platform makes more sense. Instead of sinking costs into artists who may or may not break, why not open up the platform to allow more content in and let users vote it up – make it to the "frontpage" of any label enough times, and you could land more promotional resources or production help.

Just like Buzzfeed, labels don't need to be constrained by false scarcity anymore. Imagine if radio were to open up and adopt a Buzzfeed like system that allowed users to control some of the content, alongside the DJs. Resources once spent on radio promotion would be freed up for other uses. Passive listeners could still sit back and tune in, whereas active listeners could play a bigger role in determining playlists. This is a radical idea and almost certainly won't happen anytime really soon, but it's coming.

As I've said before, labels need to increase the amount of content they release as well. Buzzfeed puts up an avalanche of posts every day – some well-researched and serious, others light and quick. There's room to release both a serious track from a respected artist with great production values, and a goofy chorus from a band that recorded it in the back of a van on a smartphone.

The other area where Buzzfeed's strategy can help inform labels is in the relationships with brands. Buzzfeed says it makes all its money on "sponsored content" – if you see a listicle about dogs, chances are that it is sponsored by Purina (or a similar company). We've seen artists collaborate closely with brands before (the Chris Brown Wrigley's jingle springs to mind), but why not go further and just transfer all the costs to the brand, with permission to use the label's platform. This isn't another version of Green Label Sound (the Mountain Dew label) – this is pick-your-major's release, underwritten entirely by Chase Bank. It's good exposure for the brands and more money for the labels and the artists.

The one big risk for labels adopting this model is quality control. While Buzzfeed has done a reasonably good job at this, in some cases deleting old posts that didn't measure up to new standards, other imitator sites have fallen flat. I've read articles on some of them that are so poorly written, sexist, and racist that I vow never to go back – and that's a huge danger when you have daily posting quotas to meet and basically allow anything onto your site. Then again, outrage does breed traffic, and what I think is sexist and noxious might be some bro's favorite thing ever. But assuming that someone minds the shop, going the way of Buzzfeed might be a step forward for the labels.

# What Does 2015 Hold for Spotify?

First off, caveats: I have no skin in the game, really, when it comes to Spotify's success or failure. I pay for, use, and generally like the service, but I don't work for them (never have) and have no financial stake in the company. I'm also using "Spotify" as a more or less generic term in this piece; much of what I am writing could be applied to Beats, Rdio, YouTube, etc. I use the term Spotify because it's easier than writing "streaming service" over and over, and also because it has been on the receiving end of most of the artist criticism.

I now want to say the biggest thing that Spotify can't say officially, for many reasons: artists should have no beef with Spotify. If they have beef with anyone, it should be with their labels. Spotify (presumably) signed deals with the labels in good faith. If they didn't, they should be shut down and run out of town, but because that hasn't happened, I'll go ahead and assume that the army of label lawyers consented to the deals with Spotify.

So, angry artist mob, go ahead and be pissed at your label. But also, maybe be pissed at yourself. After all, you and your team presumably signed YOUR contracts in good faith (although we've all seen enough episodes of Behind the Music to know this isn't the case sometimes). You gotta read the fine print, though. You can't use your friend's cousin who just passed the bar to save a few bucks. If you think your lawyer sucked, I urge you to report them and then see if Sarah Koenig wants to do a Serial series about you.

I'm saying this because I know Spotify has to play nice with the labels and artists and can't come right out and tell people to back off. The fact that Spotify allows artists to pull their content rather than saying, "tough tits, we had a deal" is a pretty savvy PR move on their part.

This all came up for me again because an indie artist I really like pulled his music off Spotify for no coherent reason. The best he could offer was that it wasn't "artist friendly," but his music is all over YouTube and Soundcloud, so...basically, he doesn't know what he's talking about. He then linked out to an interview with another indie musician who defended Soundcloud (which pays nothing, for the most part) while ripping on Spotify (which pays more than nothing).

The other insanely frustrating thing about all of this is that no one seems to be offering any other solutions. It's like hating Obamacare – if you offer a solution like a single payer system, that's constructive and moves the conversation forward. If you stand around and scream "death panels! witchcraft! SOCIALISM!," eh, not so much.

And no, a time machine back to 1999 isn't a solution. CDs aren't the solution. iTunes isn't the solution. Vinyl is really not the solution, and I've gone from being someone who liked vinyl to being someone who wanted to bang my head against a wall when I heard "vinyl is back" for the millionth time. Jack White is not here to save you, people. If anything, judging by recent appearances, he wants to drink your blood and then compress your bones into a 7-inch.

Not liking streaming is fine. Not liking Spotify's payout model is fine. Tell everyone how to make it better. Want to explore building a streaming service as an artist-owned collective rather than a private company? That's probably not the solution in the long term, but at least it's a new idea.

Streaming isn't going away, at least right now. Ten years from now we'll have chips implanted in our brains to take care of all this, but for now, this is what we've got. And as Spotify continues to grow, it's just going to own more of the means of production.

Maybe this was all a very long intro to the other 2015 prediction I alluded to last week – that Spotify will launch a "label" and just start releasing content on their own. Unless they have a clause in their label deals that prohibits this (and I don't know, but it's not outside the realm of possibility), it would be a great move for them to find a big artist at the end of a contract cycle and swoop right in. They could also sign a bunch of up-and-coming acts, and they probably should to at least test things out, but then they need to go get a star and fire the first shot.

Netflix has done this, and done it really well. There are probably a fair amount of people who signed up to the service to watch "House of Cards" and then never bothered to cancel, or decided they loved it and binge watched Scandal (me). Amazon has done the same with many authors, and I can only see the trend continuing across formats.

The real test will be whether music can stay windowed forever, or if people will pay for multiple services just to hear a handful of different albums. I pay for Netflix and cable, and also have Amazon Prime, but I don't pay for Hulu because the content isn't compelling enough for me. Other than free trials, I've never used multiple streaming services, but if my favorite band on earth put out something that I could only get on Beats, I might be tempted.

This will all shake out in 2015, and probably in the coming years. A source at a label told me they project that streaming will become dominant in 2017 or 2018, so we still have a few more years until we catch up with the Nordics. But the trend is clear, and artists need to make sure they're fully educated about what side of history they want to be on.

## Don't Want No Short Short Songs

I wrote a bit last week about why the album format continues to exist; now I want to rip apart the song format. I just skimmed a playlist on Spotify and most of the songs clock in at around three and a half minutes. I would guess that since the birth of pop and definitely since the rise of commercial radio, the vast majority of pop, rock, country, and hip-hop songs have generally come in somewhere between the three and four minute mark. This makes sense in terms of being able to program stations in blocks between ads and in terms of being able to play enough different artists to keep listeners engaged.

For fifty-odd years, this formula has worked just fine. There were always outliers on the margins (punk bands compressing songs into thirty second blasts; experimental acts and jam bands noodling out twenty minute tunes), but for the most part, people followed the rules. We all knew, generally, what a song "was."

But that doesn't mean we liked it. Radio stations used to call people and play seven-second clips of tracks they were considering adding; if an audience didn't love those seven seconds, the track was unlikely to make it into rotation. Anyone who has ever driven around with me has seen me fly up and down the radio dial, giving each track a cursory chance before moving on, and I know I'm not the only person to do this. Apple introduced thirty second clips of songs on iTunes, because that's all you need to hear to decide if you like something enough to buy it; Spotify reports that one in four songs get skipped before the five second mark.

To me, this points to the fact that listeners want something shorter, more akin to the length of Vine or Instagram videos, than the standard verse-chorus-verse-solo-chorus etc etc format that they've been served for the past several years. But this would also force a radical reimagining of what a song actually looks like.

Some musicians are starting to move in this direction, releasing clips and stems of tracks and asking listeners to remix them and create unique tracks. A startup called Muzooka has released a "Tinder for music" discovery platform, where people can swipe left and right based on a ten second clip (full disclosure, I worked for Muzooka). But both of these drop users off in the same place we've been for ages – in the case of remix contests, the winners are usually released as a standard full track; with Muzooka, you add the songs you swipe to a playlist and then unlock a longer version of the track.

What I'm interested in is taking this a step further and re-examining why we need to release "songs" in the first place. I know this is weird and radical and won't happen any time soon. But just as I argued last week that artists need to get outside the box of album cycles and focus on just getting music out to the masses, I'll argue this week that they need to focus on getting everything out to the masses. Maybe it's an awesome hook. Maybe it's a verse. Maybe it's something they've been noodling on for a while and want feedback on. It can be ten seconds or a minute. But it needs to be something.

Again, I realize this won't happen in the near future. But take a look at what is happening in TV and film – kids are moving away from the weekly, produced, half-hour to hour format, and getting much more interested in the short, fast, slightly more amateurish YouTube style content. It's about volume, not necessarily quality – a few bad episodes could really ding a TV series, whereas a few bad videos will just sink to the bottom of a YouTube channel and allow better content to rise.

Some artists will rise to this challenge, and others won't. I don't see Wilco starting to release weird, short snippets anytime soon. And I still think, especially among older consumers, there will be a desire for the traditional song structure. But there also needs to be a recognition that we should broaden the concept of what a song is to include other formats and concepts. The mold needs to keep expanding or it'll just wind up breaking.

## Does Rihanna Need a Union Card?

For the past few weeks, I've been extolling the idea that artists should be producing content all the time. Releasing songs, videos, Vines, funny clips – anything to stay in the public eye and keep your name in circulation. I've praised the savvy sex tape, the artfully constructed "nip-slip," and the notion that all press is good press. This week, I want to come at it from a different angle and probably contradict myself – because within all these discussions, we've forgotten that the artist in question is a laborer, working to create art.

I have a dim memory of Eddie Vedder talking about touring in Rolling Stone, and saying something to the effect of "it's fun work, but it's work." Getting on stage every night, whether you want to or not, is work. And forget half-assing your set – miss a line and it'll be all over YouTube the next day. I went to some shows ten years ago where the bands were either too wasted (Modest Mouse) or too...something (Cat Power) to perform – I don't think anyone would put up with that now. You gotta be on, all the time.

Artists have to be on all the time in their social lives as well. The highest tier of artists always lived in the public eye, although in the age before everyone had a camera and immediate access to tabloids and social networks, there was the off-chance of striking a deal with the media for a quiet dinner or an uninterrupted playground session with the kids. Now every minute is fair game. Not only that, the artist has to create all their own extra content, in the form of tweets and Facebook posts and Vines and Snapchats and...

I use the term "the social second shift," because for many people (not just artists) keeping up your brand online has become a second job. The original second shift work (cooking, cleaning) is now easily outsourced thanks to many of the same app developers and VCs who gave us the social apps – I can press a few buttons and have prepared food, groceries, a house cleaner, and a babysitter at my door in moments. All the time I would have spent cleaning, I spend tweeting.

For artists, this is all magnified, because the thirst for content from them is so great. I praised Miley Cyrus recently for her sharp handling of her social image, but I also wonder if she ever takes a night off. Lady Gaga started out as a character played by Stefani Germanotta, but she eventually morphed into her alter-ego full time. When I spoke to her a few years ago, I asked her if she ever took a few days off and wore khakis or something, and she said she never did.

Part of the reason we have trouble talking about artists and labor is that it's very hard to define what we mean by "labor." Sure, there's recording, and performing, and even modeling and acting if that's something they do, but what about everything else? What about inhabiting a persona day in and day out? What about talking to fans, and taking selfies, and posting photos on Instagram? Is that labor, or just the cost of doing business? It's easy when we define the product of labor as a car; it's much harder when we define the product of labor as a star?

Some of this is due to the fact that we, as a society, see art and music as inessential luxuries, and don't think we need to pay for them in the end. People make noise about wanting artists to be compensated, but Napster was able to succeed because plenty of people thought it was OK to get art for free. Making a living as an artist is still seen as pipe dream and a luxury, not a viable career path. Imagine a child telling their parent they wanted to be a firefighter when they grew up, and the parent asking about "backup plans" or telling them "not everyone can make it." Now imagine the response if the child says they want to be a musician, or an artist.

I often think about what an artists union would look like. I should point out that the American Federation of Musicians does some great lobbying work but certainly isn't as big as it needs to be. A number of classical musicians and symphonies are members of unions, as are backup dancers. But a bigger, more powerful union for musicians would be a game changer. First, there would be age limits, so the face of teen pop would be altered – but kids would no longer be sold to the machine by momagers. Second, there would be far more transparency around contracts – ideal in the age of Spotify, when no one seems to understand what they are signing. Collective bargaining for artists could help provide a benefits and a living wage for all musicians. Not everyone would qualify, but maybe it could be set up like the Screen Actors Guild – play a minimum numbers of shows, or get a minimum number of streams, and you're in.

This still doesn't solve the broader issue of how we define labor when it comes to artists like Rihanna and Lady Gaga, who not only work like fiends but exist in the public eye. Maybe fans at least need to step back and realize the need for a social contract, that they are now owed access all the time. Maybe artists need to put up a few more walls, put away the phones, and give themselves a forty hour week once in awhile.

## The Death of the Musical Middle Class

With the publication of Ethan Kaplan's totally brilliant "Generic Article About Spotify" a few weeks ago, I thought we'd truly hit the limit on how many ways we could skin the streaming cat. But alas, here's comes noted old white man and Pink Floyd member Nick Mason in NME to complain about Spotify (and Apple. How cute, he thinks it's 2006!). They don't pay artists. They "devalue" music. Only one more cliche and I get a bingo!

Here's what this is really about, and here's why the people who complain about streaming tend to fit a certain profile – they used to make tons of money off music, now they don't, and that's not OK. They love to trot out the idea of the "middle-class artist" as something that needs to be preserved at all costs. Here's the problem – soon there won't be any middle class artists, because soon there won't be any middle class, period.

Now, that sucks. I was raised by boomer parents who got jobs right after they finished college and proceeded to do those jobs for thirty-odd years, until they retired with pensions and benefits. I just went home to visit and they are loving life right now. Meanwhile, everyone I know under thirty (and a fair amount of people I know under forty) are working two or three gigs and paying for Obamacare, just to get by. They've had two or three careers already, and a couple of jobs within each. They jump around and pick stuff up where they can. At one time, only a certain subset of people had hyphenated jobs ("actress-waitress," "model-bartender," etc); now almost everyone does.

The worst part about it is that we're still teaching kids to focus on picking lifetime career paths. I spoke to an eighteen year old college freshman yesterday, and she was worried about what she wanted to be when she grew up. I'm almost twice her age, and I'm still not sure about that – or if that's even a concept that matters anymore. Rather than focusing on building out a set of core competencies that can be broadly applied to different industries, people are still laser focused on being "something" (a journalist, a programmer, a musician, etc).

I also gave a guest lecture for a college class and a student asked me if I thought music sales would ever come back. They won't. We're never getting the music industry of the nineties back, just like we're never getting the manufacturing industry of the fifties back.

But there's an upside – there are more ways than ever to make money as a musician these days. An indie band will never sell a ton of albums, but they can license a track for a commercial. Being in a cool band in your twenties can get you in the door at a hip agency in your thirties. Many brands and startups want to have music experts on their teams, and while teaching kids to play the same four chords over and over isn't most people's dream job, it's an income source.

We have to get over the notion of the old musical middle class, where you could put out an album every two years, do a bunch of tour dates, sell some t-shirts, and make $75,000 a year. The new reality looks like driving for Lyft when you're home, maybe taking a few freelance composing gigs for an ad agency, releasing and touring around your own music, and bartending at your buddy's place on weekends. Is this less fun, perhaps, or more stressful, than the old way? Absolutely. But it's also the new normal.

As I stated above, there's a reason most of the artists who speak out against Spotify fit a certain demo – it's because they were the ones who had access to the "good old days," and then lost it. They are mostly white, generally older, and came up making music in a system that paid them well. They had something that they felt they had a right to, they lost it, and now they're pissed.

But it's worthwhile to question why so few rappers, or international artists, or younger artists, are making the same arguments. Maybe they feel beholden to Spotify or don't want to piss anyone off. But it's just as likely that they never would have had access to the middle class artist life anyway, and that the new order actually helps them get their music out. Do you honestly think Psy could have been Psy ten years ago?

When people talk about the gig economy as a new concept, it's because it's a new concept for a very select group of people. Women, immigrants, and people of color have always been part of the gig economy, not because it was cool and freeing and driving for Lyft is a super fun way to make money while finishing their novels – it was because they had no other options. Being able to "follow your passion" and make art for a living is a very class-based concept – most people are just working to pay the bills, and the idea that you have a right to write and perform music and make a living doing so is a foreign concept.

I absolutely believe in paying people for their work, but figuring out what they should be paid (or have a right to be paid) is tricky. But opposing Spotify, in the absence of a realistic solution, is just silly and privileged. I'd love to be a (middle class, educated) boomer riding life out on a cushy retirement package...but that's not an option anymore. Rather than bemoaning the lost past, we need to focus on making the gig economy more sustainable for everyone.

# Old Men Lose, Young Girls Win

After the Ray Rice story first broke, a blog I was reading encouraged readers to turn off football altogether. The reasoning was pretty simple – the ratings people can't distinguish hate-watchers from the people who are legit psyched to watch the game. Advertisers still mostly look at raw numbers when determining where to spend money, and this seems to have given rise to a wave of "made-for-Twitter" programming that people will love to hate watch (ever more award shows, Peter Pan Live with the girl from Girls and Christopher Walken, Grumpy Cat vs Sharknado, etc).

There's still no way to determine viewer intent, and this is something Miley Cyrus understands better than anyone. In the past several years, she's figured out the secret sauce of keeping attention focused on her, and making it pay off. She stays just the right side of the outrage line, and she's laughing all the way to the bank.

A note of clarification, if you're too lazy to look at her Wikipedia – Cyrus is 22 years old. She waited until she was a full-grown adult to swing around naked on a wrecking ball, but she also realized that in many minds, she's still a teenager. Remember those innocent days in 2008 when she posed for Vanity Fair wrapped in a sheet, and even though you couldn't see anything, people still freaked out? It was the first sign of the genius at work.

Since then, she's kept herself in the public eye steadily, and made all her content readily available for listening or viewing, regardless of the viewer's intent. Want to listen to her music or watch her twerk? It's all there, for free, in seconds. And it doesn't matter if the viewer is seeing red, because Miley is only seeing green. She gets paid for every view and every stream, no matter if it's a hate-watch or not. And she's figured out how's it going to go in the future – curiosity may kill the cat, but it's going to save the music biz.

Back in the old days, when you had to actually make an effort beyond typing a few words into a browser in order to check something out, Cyrus's shtick might not have worked as well. It worked for Madonna, but she was a much bigger and more established star by the time she released "Sex." Now anyone can see something on Cyrus on Good Morning America, and within seconds listen to her album or watch her videos. As long as she keeps the machine rolling, and doesn't stray too far off the path, she'll be set for a while.

Cyrus, I should point out, isn't the only star to do this – Kim Kardashian has raised this to an art form, and Rihanna seems to be adept at it as well. The age of the curiosity-driven pop star is upon us, and we're going to be more artists calibrating their lives for maximum clicks.

****

In an early Christmas present to young music writers everywhere, the New York Times released yet another "old man yells at cloud about how the music biz was better back in the day" op-ed.

The piece was written by an "online record dealer," which is a little like having a cattle rancher pen an op-ed about why beef is great and chicken will kill you. But aside from that obvious problem, the pretense of the piece is nuts: people who run record labels are the ones who should tell the public what to listen to; there's just so much bad music on the internet we need these smart men to program our playlists for us.

First off, the labels are hardly infallible – setting aside the old straw men like the Beatles and Nirvana, labels put out a whole lot of garbage as well. I grew up in the Northwest in the nineties, and remember when every dude with a guitar and a heroin problem was getting signed - it wasn't pretty. And God forbid you happened to be a talented woman, or person of color, or person whose style didn't fit with what was marketable at the moment – there was no hope for you.

Second, the web has opened up the means of distribution – and greatly reduced the reliance of people like record store clerks when it comes to telling people just what they should listen to. The author makes note of this in the most perfunctory way possible, stating: "And I suppose it is wonderful, in a way, that the music of some 16-year-old kids in Chicago, say, can be heard in Malaysia with one mouse click."

But really, in his mind, it's not, because who cares if some non-Western POC can hear music – most of that music is crap! I mean, sure, crap is subjective and all – but it's not Led Zeppelin, so it must suck.

It's no accident that most of these op-eds (and the Times seems to run one every few months, because even the Grey Lady is a slave to the clickbait) are penned by older white men, just as it's no great shock that most of people yelling the loudest about the evils of Spotify tend to be old white guys as well (Taylor Swift aside, of course). The old music biz was awesome if you were a white dude – it just kinda sucked if you were a lady, or a minority, or non-Western.

Look, I get it – coming face to face with your increasing irrelevance isn't fun. But the old saw "adapt or die" has floated around for a while now for a reason. In the battle of the old man yelling into space, or the young pop starlet conquering the internet, who do you think is going to come out on top?

## Snapchatting at the Ballet

The NEA recently released the results of a ten year long study, finding that rates of attendance at arts events dropped from 2002-2012. In 2002, 39.4% of US adults attended what they define as a core arts events (opera, jazz, classical music, ballet, musical theater, plays, art museum and gallery visits); in 2008 it was 34.6% and in 2012 it was 33.4%. The declines occurred across all age groups except for those 65 and older.

On the other end of the spectrum, Drew Magary over at Deadspin wrote a piece about getting his kids to watch sports in an age of constant distraction. He admits that football is programmed perfectly to allow people to tune in and out, checking Twitter and fantasy scores during the innumerable commercial breaks and timeouts. He goes on to bemoan the endless round of new and complicated rules, and concludes that football might be done in by being over-complicated and losing the casual viewer, who just wants to watch in-between smartphone time.

I bring up both these things because I think they're interconnected, in a strange way. What younger consumers want, more than anything, is interactivity. They want all their friends to know about the show they're seeing, the game they're watching, the food they're eating. And while the older generation can bray endlessly about putting phones away and paying attention, kids don't see it like that. Instagramming a pic doesn't take anything away from whatever it is they're supposed to be paying attention to – it adds to it.

Rock shows have adapted to this remarkably well. I'm old enough to remember when venues had no-camera policies – today that would seem laughable. And yeah, it's annoying to watch a show through someone else's iPhone – but it's equally annoying to be stuck behind some tall person and unable to see, or next to some drunk girl who sings along loudly. It's the cost of doing business.

Other forms of live music and theater haven't caught on. Taking out your cellphone at the opera, the ballet, or the symphony is tantamount to standing up and starting the wave. You can maybe sneak in a quick tweet or pic before the curtain goes up, and then you go into a black hole. And while you can check your phone in most museums, many also forbid taking pictures of the art.

An aside: many museums are terrible user experiences, and I'm guessing they are going be disrupted in the next 10 years or so. I went to the Met a few weeks ago and it was basically a battle to get through throngs of people to maybe glance at a painting for five seconds before getting pushed away. With the rise of better, clearer screens, I'd honestly prefer to spend time examining a painting on my tablet than standing in line for hours just to look at the Mona Lisa for almost no time. Inactive exhibits are great and non-replicable experiences, but I think the standard "shuffle around and stare at paintings behind a rope" experience is not long for this earth.

Another aside, then back to music: movie theaters are just as bad, and as soon as studios start releasing on-demand and charging $20 to let people watch when they want, they'll be boarded up. I've wanted to see "Wild" for the last few weeks, but the screening times at my local theater are inconvenient; I want to be able to stop and restart if I please; and most importantly, I want to socialize. Again, screens in a theater will get you booted. But I want to be able to text all my friends who have equally strong feelings about it, because that sharing is a big part of the experience for me.

Back to music – if opera, classical, etc want to grow their younger audiences, they have to make their content more shareable. As beautiful as I find Lincoln Center and Carnegie Hall, maybe they're not the best venues for these performances all the time. Concerts in the park are a great place to start, but I think performing non-traditional pieces in non-traditional spaces would be a great way to attract younger viewers.

The length of many of these events is another issue. I know this will lead to much pearl clutching, but most operas are too long. I like the opera, but asking someone to sit for four hours is a lot to ask, especially from kids who are used to constant movement and interaction. I don't have a great solution, aside from editing the programs, and I realize that will take away a lot of elements of the story.

Another idea is to make these types of media less event-focused. One of the main reasons cited in the NEA study that people give for not attending performances is that they lack someone to attend with. Offering a live stream of the event where people could pay to watch from home is a suggestion I've long offered for rock events, and it could work for classical events as well. Using new media to reach out to younger audiences (a Snapchat story about art) is always worthwhile, and making events easier to share could keep younger audiences engaged.

It all boils down to this – we now almost always have the option to do something else if what we're currently consuming isn't holding our interest. I'm not a big fan of forcing people to sit through something just for the sake of perceived moral fortitude – I'd much rather meet them halfway to give them an enjoyable, if non-traditional, experience. If you keep forcing people to consume content only on your terms, pretty soon you'll just force them away.

# Sign this label deal or we'll shoot this dog

Like everyone else, I read Zoe Keating's blog post about YouTube Music Key's contracts last week. I was a little turned off by her "I'm a struggling artist! Who met Eric Schmidt at Davos last year!" vibe, but I'll give her credit for shining some light on the inner workings of these deals. From my vantage point, the deal YouTube is offering isn't bad – they're helping artists monetize, claim their work, and make sure their catalog is complete. If artists want a real alternative to Spotify, Music Key could be the solution. At minimum, having another strong player in the market will create competition, which artists can then use to their advantage to negotiate better deals. A monopoly in the streaming space helps no one.

I also spent some time last weekend watching the flawed-but-still-interesting "Sonic Highways." The Seattle episode was one of the better ones, but when I saw the inevitable picture of Nirvana on the cover of Rolling Stone with Kurt in his "Corporate Magazines Still Suck" shirt, I felt...rage.

Because here's the thing with these contracts – artists don't have to sign them. I'll say it one more time, for emphasis – if someone presents you with a contract you don't like YOU. DON'T. HAVE. TO. SIGN. IT.

No one forced Nirvana to sign to Geffen back in the day. All members of the band were adults who made the choice freely and decided to put their signatures on paper. They could have stayed on Sub Pop and grown into a respected indie band. They could have quit the band, gone back to school, and had other jobs. They weighed the pro's and con's and took the money. So it now rings a little hollow when I hear interviews with Kurt Cobain talking about how much he hates being a rock star, because no one made him become one. And yes, I know he struggled with depression and substance abuse and that clouded his thinking, but being smart enough to engineer posing on the cover of Rolling Stone while dissing corporate magazines is the very definition of having your cake and eating it too, and you gotta be of sound and savvy mind to pull that off.

As for Zoe Keating, if she finds the YouTube contract unsatisfying, she can and should refuse to sign it. If an artist wants to keep their music off streaming, that's their decision, although I personally think it's a silly one. But if you want to release your music on flash drives hidden around the world and have your fans go on scavenger hunts to find them, or only release CDs at Target, or whatever, that's your prerogative. If you're willing to accept that fewer people will hear what you're working on, or discover you, or that you'll likely make less money, fine.

Some people have said that Google is acting as an 800lb gorilla in this situation, and they are totally right. And water is wet, and snow is cold. Sometimes little guys have to deal with big, heartless companies if they want to accomplish a certain thing. I would love to have a custom mortgage that worked just for me, but Wells Fargo doesn't offer that. My husband and I weighed the decision of signing a deal that we didn't love against the benefit of owning our apartment, and came down on the side of ownership being a higher priority for us. Other people might decide the benefit doesn't outweigh the cost and keep renting, or look for another deal.

I've been seeing a lot of non-music tech articles that that all seem to have the same general theme: "why can't I have everything I want exactly when I want it?" I watched a woman throw a fit because she couldn't bring her toddler into a bar a while back. I heard another person complain about not getting promoted at work because he left at 5pm to go running every day.

Guess what – you don't always get what you want all the time. You get the toddler OR the bar. You get the promotion OR you get to take off and go the gym whenever you want. There's no "right" choice in any of those scenarios, but there are choices.

So if you want your music to reach millions of people, you might have to sign a label deal whose terms you don't love. You might have to play nice with streaming partners you find distasteful. You might have to do boring interviews with inept journalists, or play concerts when you're jetlagged or hungover, or wear dumb outfits and dye your hair and shill for products. If you don't like, nobody's forcing you to do any of it. In the old days, with very limited distribution pathways, it was a little harder to go it alone; now, it's a million times easier to make your own rules if you don't love the options in front of you.

But it's really not worth using a deal you don't like as a personal brand building exercise. If you hate major labels, sign to an indie. Release music by yourself. Drive an Uber and rent your place on AirBNB when you're on the road and play small clubs. Will you make millions of dollars and headline Coachella? No. But if what you have to do to get there is antithetical to your beliefs, then those things won't make you happy anyway.

## Music Tech's Long, Cold Winter

I've started hearing rumblings of an artist backlash against Soundcloud's plans to monetize by putting audio ads at the start of tracks. The logic of all this is a little curious – how do artists, who presumably want to get paid, think Soundcloud is going to make money? Magic? Sorting out who gets what from the massive numbers of remixes and covers on Soundcloud is going to take a ton of time, and I expect many DJs are going to feel dissatisfied when it's all over. Some have predicted that this might be a bad year for Soundcloud, and while I'm reserving judgement, they seem to have lost their way a bit recently.

In fact, most of music tech seems to be in a funk right now. Streaming just seems to chug along, with Spotify becoming ever-more-dominant (my guess is that Jay-Z will wind up selling WiMP to them at some point; those Nordic subscribers are probably worth some money). Beats is in limbo until we hear more from Apple, and other services will probably consolidate or disappear. Meanwhile, I still talk to plenty of people who are perfectly happy to just use Pandora and suffer through a few ads in order to have background music all the time. Some smaller companies are doing some cool things (including the company that I work for, Muzooka; look for an announcement soon), but overall, things feel kind of stale.

I'd love to go back and take the 30,000 foot view for a minute – what problems are we solving, exactly? In terms of distribution, streaming has likely come as far as it's going to without some pretty big structural changes. All-you-can-eat music is pretty worthless without affordable, universal data coverage, but there's nothing Spotify can do about that. Wi-fi enabled cars appear to be even closer (I fell for the Chevy ad during the Superbowl as well) but we're still far away from a connected world. The biggest problems are still structural – my beautiful iPhone 6, my lifeline to the world, is still useless when I'm overseas or in certain parts of Manhattan.

I've often said that streaming is going to wind up being just another format in a long line of formats for music distribution, but now I think it's going to stick around longer than I originally thought. I might be the only person on earth who is sad that Google Glass flopped, not because the current iteration looked good or had any real promise, but because of what it represented. It could have led to a world of radical transparency, where the whole world really was watching, and listening, and paying attention. I still think seeing the world through another person's eyes is a great concept, and could have been huge for music. I could have clicked on a livestream of a show down the block, or half a world away. I could have watched music being made in real time, or seen what it's like to play for a crowd of thousands. Maybe Glass was just too early for its own good.

The live space still seems oversaturated and underserved, with enough apps to tell me what bands are in town on any given evening to fill a phone, but very few to tell me which I'll like or help me have an enjoyable experience. Most venues continue to focus on attracting a younger crowd without realizing just how much money they're leaving on the table by not hosting shows that start earlier and feature some creature comforts. I'd also still love to be able to just put on a show in the background and see what a certain band sounds like live before I commit to seeing them, or watch a show I missed because of a work or family commitment.

What I'm most excited about are innovations outside of the music space, and how they'll impact how we consume music and other content in the future. Twitter was in no way a music app and yet it has radically revolutionized the way we interact with artists; ditto YouTube, Instagram, Vine, etc. Right now I'm really interested in mobile payments startups, mostly because waiting in line at stores is an unnecessary waste of time in this day and age. Will the ability to pay with a click have any impact on how we consume music, especially now that we've moved away from purchasing physical copies of albums anyway? Certainly concert tickets could be sold via codes on posters and ads, and of course merch sales would be easier than ever. One-click IRL shopping also allows for more impulse buying – people waiting in long lines often just give up and decide they don't really need an item, and mobile payments reduce that friction.

People also hate on the sharing economy, sometimes with good reason, but it could have transformative effects on how artists tour and make music. There's an "Airbnb for gear" now, which could allow many more low-income artists to start making music and even touring. The sharing economy also allows artists to monetize their apartments and cars when on the road, providing a nice little income boost.

Will the next big thing in music come from inside the space, or somewhere totally unexpected? I don't know, but I do hope something cool comes soon – it's getting a little dull over here.

# The World Is Flat

I travel internationally a handful of times a year, and each trip usually has a few "the world is flat" moments. I talked baseball with a cab driver in Japan! I flew to Africa and wound up in a hipster motorcycle shop/coffee bar just like the one three blocks from my house! I watched a movie, starring French people, about young artists in Brooklyn, in Paris. Basically, every trip I have a handful of those moments where I think "we're all connected. Deep down, we're just humans! Borders are just social constructs (drawn by British men after wars, sometimes)."

But while all this is lovely, and should definitely get me a New York Times column and a book deal, it doesn't quite translate when it comes to music and entertainment and tech. The west (which I'm defining here mostly as the US, Canada, and the UK) export the lion's share of music and film culture to the rest of the world – and we don't really reciprocate. Even with all our connectivity, our more open and fluid digital culture, non-English speaking acts are still categorized as "other" in the US.

That doesn't mean they can't reach some level of success – Juanes, for example, sells out Madison Square Garden and the Staples Center. But only one critic out of hundreds surveyed voted for him in the Village Voice Pazz and Jop Poll last year. Maybe it wasn't a great record (full disclosure – I'm not a huge fan myself) but it was a big release for many people. I've been to some Latin shows, and I'm probably one of a small group who doesn't speak any Spanish. Ditto for the K-Pop show I attended a few years back – the audience was almost entirely Korean, Korean-American, a few nerdy white dudes, and me.

Meanwhile, Western artists can go to Seoul and pack clubs, despite not speaking the language. Taylor Swift can sell out any arena in the world, but the Taylor Swift of China, or Russia, or Brazil would only attract a niche audience in the US, unless she sang the bulk of her songs in English. And even then, she'd still be boxed in as a "fill-in-the-blank-ethnicity star" rather than just a pop star.

We're more mixed and more connected than ever, and yet the default in almost all genres remains Western and English-speaking. Part of this is dependent on how widely spoken English is in many parts of the world, whereas in the US, learning a second language if you're a native English speaker is seen as a privilege, not the norm. Part of it is the high regard in which many people still hold American culture – I've visited every continent except Antarctica, and when I mentioned I lived in Williamsburg, everyone know what that meant. People love New York and Brooklyn everywhere.

But this myopia has downsides for music, tech, and the music biz. If we're so hung up on English-speaking artists and "othering" everyone else, we're missing out on some amazing music. K-Pop's not my thing, but it's incredible to watch and could have big implications for Western pop artists if they were influenced by it. There's probably some smoking hot singer in a developing country right now who could make a label millions of dollars and sell a ton of soda in some great branding deal – but because labels have a narrow view of talent, they'll miss out.
Tech suffers from this as well – many of the problems tech companies solve are those endemic to the Bay Area and New York. Which isn't to say some can't become global brands – Facebook and Twitter are the most obvious cases here. But if we limit our scope to first world problems, we miss out on opportunities to solve even bigger issues and potentially disrupt massive industries.

I'm not talking about taking all the bros coding away at apps to deliver your dry cleaning and tasking them with solving malaria, either (although that's a good idea). One startup I'm obsessed with right now is Snapscan, out of South Africa – it's an app that allows you to settle a bill by snapping a QR code. Because mobile commerce is so huge in Africa, it's been able to thrive in its home market, while companies that have tried to do this in the US have failed. But if Snapscan or another firm like it succeeded, it could disrupt payment as we know it – no more waiting in line at the grocery store (or the merch table, to bring it back to music). You could buy tickets by snapping a code on a poster. Hear an artist's music in an ad, take a pic of the screen, and donate a few bucks.

I'm really fascinated by the next emerging markets, like India, China, and Nigeria (specifically Lagos). My hope is that we can develop a two-way music and culture exchange – these markets have tons of young people and are primed to consume music from the west, but they also have a ton of talented artists who influences are totally different than those of kids in US. A few episodes ago on Broad City, Ilana envisioned a future where we're all "caramel and queer;" hopefully music can be integrated globally by then.

## The Label-Less Future

Two interesting music/tech news tidbits came across the wires this morning, seemingly unrelated. The first is that Snapchat, which I know is more than a platform for topless teen selfies these days, is interested in partnering with Apple to buy Big Machine. The snarky part of me feels like Evan Spiegel is doing this to hook up with/get back together with Taylor Swift, but the more I thought about, the more it kind of made sense. More on that below.

The other big story is the supposed launch of QTrax (hello 2008!) with a totally free, ad-supported, Facebook style model. Much like Beyond Oblivion, QTrax is best known for throwing awesome parties and never launching, and also for lying about having deals with labels. But now they are promising a release with 30% of equity going to artists and no paid tiers, claiming that Facebook is able to rely completely on ads, and they should be able to as well.

Here's the flaw in that logic, though: Facebook doesn't pay any of their content creators. All my photos and posts and funny comments on links are done for free. I also don't get paid to tweet or post photos on Instagram. I find myself more drawn to my social media feeds than my blog feeds, especially on weekends and holidays, because blogs don't update that often. This is a good thing in theory – bloggers are employees and should have time off – but if I just want to consume content, my Instagram feed is better bet than my Pulse feed at any given time.

Here's the sneaky/brilliant/messed up (depending on your perspective) thing about all these companies – they amass tons of content and don't have to pay a dime. I'm not a great Instagram photographer (OK, I'm actually pretty bad), but there are people out there who are, and Instagram still doesn't pay them anything. They make money tangentially, from other companies. The most famous dogs on Instagram aren't making money on their photos – they're making money doing product placements and appearances. Ditto for Twitter; while they might have thrown some cash at celebs in the early days, they probably haven't paid out anyone in ages, because they don't need to. People can just make money by having big followings on Twitter, but if they are getting paid to actually write tweets, it's by someone else.

So, if we follow this logic, what's not to say the next step isn't just using socials to distribute music and using that as a platform to make money doing other things (touring, endorsements, etc)? Soundcloud was arguably at the forefront of this – tons of people were willing to post their music for free and then try to make money elsewhere. The problem was mostly with the user experience – Soundcloud never got as big as any of the other social platforms and never quite became the place for music discovery. Maybe if they'd built in a Pandora-like functionality they could have cracked a more mainstream audience.

Part of what hampered Soundcloud was the fact that they had to deal with a copyright system that hasn't caught up with the new digital reality. I say this as someone who believes in copyright but also knows that it can stand in the way of creativity. Presenting someone else's work as your own is obviously wrong, but sampling and remixing are greyer areas, and on a platform like Soundcloud, you can get bogged down pretty quickly.

This all brings me back around to Snapchat and Apple and Big Machine, and why if this deal happens, it could be groundbreaking. There would be no more third parties standing in the way, and the content could flow directly from the creator to the audience, with the artist monetizing off ancillary revenue streams. I've long advocated for streaming services to do direct deals with artists, and this could be first in a number of deals between creators and platforms.

Even if the Snapchat deal does happen, things won't change for a while. Outside the digital music bubble, there are plenty of people still buying CDs and listening to terrestrial radio, and labels still control radio promotions with an iron fist. But kids these days are sneaky, and consuming content in very different ways. A woman who hosts goofy YouTube shows is just as famous with teens as a boy-band star. Snippets of content (seven second videos, 140 characters tweets) are as important as three minute pop songs. Audio quality is a low priority – explain the Pono player to a teenager and they'll just laugh.

I don't think QTrax will succeed because, come on, it's QTrax, and because it's too early. We've got at least another generation before everything turns into wonderful nineties-era DIY dream where we're all just creating and swapping content on the side, and making money other ways.

\*\*\*\*

The other big recent Apple news is the self-driving car, which I would buy as soon as it came off the lot, because I bet it'll be awesome. Again, it's still a ways out, but here's my hot take on the matter: the self driving car will kill terrestrial radio. Most people listen to the radio in the car because they want traffic reports (which won't matter if Waze is driving you) and because they can't do anything else in the car – read, text, etc (or at least, they shouldn't do these things). Self driving cars mean that you can read the paper rather than listening to snippets of news between songs. It means you can scroll through feeds, or play games, or watch TV or movies – all of which will compete with music for your time. Of all the things that will be disrupted by self-driving cars, including millions of jobs, radio is low on the totem pole – but worth watching regardless.

# How to Make Live Music Suck Less

I spent the weekend in Nashville for the Pollstar conference, and when I wasn't falling on ice (free idea: Uber for CLEARING YOUR FUCKING SIDEWALKS), I was talking to people about live music and seeing bands (and one very weird award show).

Fundamentally, the live music space is broken for many of the same reasons most of the music industry is broken – strip away all the apps and new distribution channels and nothing has changed for the past forty or so years. Venues are still generally cavernous spaces with very limited seating and bands at 9/10/11pm, with half hour breaks between each set. Buying tickets is a pain in the ass, with scalping, sites that crash all the time, and a big supply and demand mismatch for most shows. If there has ever been a show in the history of live music where the venue's capacity exactly equalled the number of people who wanted to see the show, I'd be shocked. Instead, you get sold-out shows with tons of people shut out, or undersold shows where money is lost. You've got overpriced drinks, surly bouncers, and shitty sightlines, not to mention all manner of assholes in the crowd. It's enough to make you want to spend your money on the approximately one million other options you have if you're young, have some spare cash, and live in a decent sized media market.

Live shows usually suck, and yet, when they're great, they're brilliant. I did some back of the envelope math and I've seen probably about a thousand live shows in my time, and can recall maybe twenty or thirty of them with any real clarity. But seeing Liz Phair do "Exile in Guyville" all the way through, or PJ Harvey play the old Knitting Factory, or Lykke Li play for a hundred executives at Mercury Lounge...it's pretty goddamn amazing. So I keep going, hoping that out of all the terrible to forgettable bands I slog through, there will be another memorable show.

All this said, here are some ways to change the live experience for the better:

**Make the shows easier to find.** When I was getting ready to go to Nashville last weekend, I thought I'd see if any good bands were playing while I was there. Sounds easy enough. After a bunch of time digging through their local alt-weekly's site, I gave up – I couldn't get the information I needed to establish whether or not any bands I liked (or would like) were playing. And I'm a pretty big music fan, and willing to do the research.

There are apps for this, of course, like Songkick and Bandsintown. But how about syncing up a TripIt account with a ticketing company that can then tell me what shows I might like to check out while I'm traveling. I'd also love to be able to see a list of what the most-buzzed-about new bands are and when they're playing my market – I already know that I like what I like, but I want to be able to see new things before they totally blow up.

**Start shows earlier.** I tried to find the blog post an artist wrote about this a while back but the internet ate it. Regardless, clubs are leaving huge amounts of money on the table by ignoring an older audience that can't stay out til midnight because they have kids and regular jobs. Start the show at 8pm, so people have enough time to get out of work and eat something, two bands on the bill (sorry, third opener, but no one is watching you anyway), quick set changes, wrap it all up by ten. Done and done.

I realize that this won't work for, say, Avicii. But for legacy acts this is a great way to cater to their fan base without making it a huge struggle for them to come out.

**Shorter transition times.** I started going to see live music in 1995. Twenty years later, with all the technological advances, it still takes half an hour between bands. And yes, I know that this is to give people time to go to the bar, because that's where clubs make their money. But it also turns away plenty of customers; go back to the blog post I wrote about the NEA study, where one of the biggest reasons people gave for avoiding events was that they had no one to go with.

I go to plenty of shows solo, just because I go to so many and it can be hard to rally someone for every gig, especially when your friends are getting older and having kids (see point above). I'm used to it and don't care all that much, but standing around by yourself for half an hour between bands blows. So plenty of people wind up skipping the show.

To deal with the smaller window for drink sales, venues can add more drink stations. The costs would be slightly higher, but better attendance would likely balance it out.

**Rethink the room.** The vast majority of live venues are big rooms with no place to sit down. That's been the way we watch live music for years, but no one has ever stopped to ask if that's the best way to watch music. I don't have a solution, but it's worth stepping back and questioning conventional wisdom. I'm a fan of venues with bleacher seats, like the old Northsix in Brooklyn; any place that allows a short person like me to get above the crowd is great.

Because the live music biz isn't imploding like the recorded music biz, it's easier to be complacent and think the money will keep rolling in. But it's also good to start looking for fixes early, so when venues find themselves behind the eight ball, they won't collapse.

****

Free piece of advice for musicians: if you want to lose a room, the easiest way to do it is by taking minute long pauses between each song. I saw this TWICE in the three days I was in Nashville. Don't do this.

# Popping the Bubble

That tech people and music people live inside rarified bubbles should come as a surprise to absolutely no one. If you've ever set foot in Silicon Valley, or Brooklyn, or Hollywood, you know just what I'm talking about – young, over-educated people jabbering on about a hot new app or band. When they leave that bubble, it's usually to marvel at how gosh-darn quaint everything is – "look, Tim, a phone that's not a smart phone." "Wow, Betty, compact discs. I thought these things disappeared ten years ago!"

I get it, and I'm as guilty as anyone. I'm in India right now (and I promise this won't be another "white person goes to India and has feels" post) and on the way here, Air France lost my bag. A conveyer belt broke in Paris, and it took three days for my stuff to finally get to me. Meanwhile, I was waiting on hold and posting tweets that took hours to answer. Ten years ago, I probably could have shrugged all this off. Now, I was furious. The last time I was in California, I rode in a car THAT DROVE ITSELF. You're telling me a conveyor belt broke and that was what screwed everything up so royally? Really?

And that's light years ahead of India, which is great in many ways but somehow hasn't figured out that roads should maybe have lanes and they're not appropriate places for cows, humans, and dogs to wander around. I know I sound like an awful spoiled Western brat, but after coming close to death by bull-hitting-car, it's a little hard not to be a tiny bit critical.

I mention all this because we, as music tech people, need to stop and recognize that we're way, way ahead of everyone else (or behind, if you're one of those people). A buddy of mine shared some work he'd done recently with me, and he found that huge numbers of people still listen to terrestrial radio. Still! With the annoying ads and silly DJs and ten song playlists, people still listen. There are times when I feel like a maniac cult leader repping streaming music apps – a better way is possible! You don't have to live like this! You can't possibly enjoy hearing that jewelry store ad again, can you?

But I guess people...do. The vast majority of the world is OK with stupid ads on the radio, with equipment that breaks and takes ages to fix, with driving next to cows. Every so often, though, something breaks through this and a new technology does really change the game. Netflix is an example of this; Uber (for better or worse) is another. But so far nothing in music has come close. Spotify has come close, but so far the only market it has managed to conquer is the Nordics – great, but not representative of the wider world.

The biggest problem facing music startups right now is not artist payouts, or label deals – it's the fact that they are just too damn insular. I've been to many streaming service offices, and most people there are under forty and live in major cities. Spotify has hundreds of people in NYC but as far as I know, only one person in Nashville. The might have campus reps at more rural schools, but those kids only focus on converting other students, not the townies.

I originally had high hopes for Beats to crack the mainstream, because their marketing played so close to the center. They had football stars and Ellen DeGeneres on their side; how better to hit middle America? Alas, they also had a too-clever-by-half product and quickly disappeared into Apple-land – it remains to be seen what their new iteration will look like, and what sort of traction it'll get. Every other company reeks of cool, which is fine if all you want to capture is that market, but I'm guessing they want bigger things.

It all comes down to this – was the lack of on-demand streaming music really that big of a problem for most people? For people like me, it was huge, and I'd be really bummed if it went away. But for most people, who still listen to the radio and have maybe shifted to Pandora...maybe it wasn't a big deal. Maybe streaming services are solving a problem where there wasn't one to begin with.

This gets back to my central point – we all need to start getting outside the bubble more. It can help us manage expectations (or make us more driven to solve problems) and it should help shape our thinking when it comes to the problems we actually need to solve. There's of course the Steve Jobs and Henry Ford school of thought that customers aren't smart enough to know what they want and need to be told what they need, but I don't think works most of the time.

All I know is this – despite everything, the world is still moving really slowly. Ubiquitous wi-fi service is still a fantasy (at least, it's my fantasy). There are no apps to track lost luggage and airlines can and will just disconnect your calls and ignore your tweets. People still shrug and listen to the morning zoo. Those of us who want to solve this would do well to realize that we've got the bring the rest of the pack with us, and find a way to communicate openly with them and show them a better way is possible. Otherwise we risk staying in our bubbles, on the grid and yet fully disconnected from reality.

## Is SXSW Too Big to Fail?

In a few days, tech folks, music biz folks, and especially music-tech folks start their annual pilgrimage to Austin for yet another SXSW. And right off the bat, I'll acknowledge that going to a cool city with nice weather to party for a few days is a dumb thing to complain about. I've talked to plenty of normal people who would be absolutely jazzed to see a ton of bands, drink free beer, and eat barbeque for a week and do it as part of their job. But for those of us in the biz, with a number of festivals under our belts, SXSW feels like the death march of fun. So many bands! And long lines! And racing all over the city before collapsing in an overpriced AirBNB, only to do it again the next day. And for what, exactly?

SXSW has gotten too big, and even worse, it's too big to fail. It bring millions of dollars to the city of Austin every year. More and bigger brands throw money at the festival, and turning money down is hard, especially when you employ a big team of people to make sure things run well. The SXSW brand has gotten so diluted that rather than being a place to discover new music and maybe get some business done, it's about seeing Lady Gaga in a vending machine, or queueing in line for Kanye's annual "secret" show, or spending half your day texting to try to schedule a meeting before your phone dies.

The festival has fallen into the classic "bigger is better" trap, outlined by Jason Fried and David Heinemeier Hansson in their book "Re/Work." Here's an example: Harvard could, with their massive endowment and vast landholdings, easily double the size of its incoming freshman class next year. Hell, they could triple or quadruple it, and make even more money. But they don't, because one of the things that makes Harvard Harvard is just how damn hard it is to get accepted. They could make a bigger profit, but they choose to protect the integrity of the brand.

SXSW didn't protect the integrity of its brand, simple as that. And now, rather than being a place that feels vital for the best minds in the tech industry and the most vibrant new artists, it's a massive free for all that feels kinda-fun (see aforementioned bands and beer) at best and obligatory at worst. For startups that don't have massive budgets, you're pretty much guaranteed to get lost in the shuffle. Part of the problem is that SXSW doesn't give companies any guidance – short of hosting a table in the convention center, there really aren't official places to go to connect with people who can help you. It just becomes a circle of people pitching each other while screaming over the music in a crowded room. And again, it's fun – but really, does your budget allow for a party week?

Music, on the other hand, has shifted away from being a business event and has become just another spring break destination. SXSW can't do much about this, but I get street-harassed more during my annual week in Austin than I do the other eleven months of the year I live in Brooklyn, and I once got groped watching a show at Stubbs. I'm honestly shocked there isn't more crime at SXSW, given the massive numbers of drunk people crammed into a relatively small space, and I guess kudos to the Austin PD for that.

For bands, SXSW seems like a bum deal. You wind up playing a ton of shows, half of which might not even be at proper venues, with no time to soundcheck and short sets. You're also up against dozens of other shows, a few of which are usually headlined by superstars. Bands this year might actually have it a little easier given the lack of banner headliners (aforementioned Kanye gig aside), but there are still too many damn shows. Most people wind up going to see bands they already know and like, or just sticking with stuff that's likely to be decent – it's easier to just sit at the Fader Fort all day and know that most of what you see will be good and buzz-worthy than to go out and take risks.

And then there are the brands, which seem more and more clueless and inappropriate every year. Converse? Makes sense. Beer sponsors? On brand. McDonalds? Really? We've hit a point where every CMO just wants to check the "millennials" box on a list and SXSW is the perfect place to do it. Just stick some buzz bands in front of a food truck (kids like those, right?) and your brand will be redeemed in the eyes of the twenty-somethings.

The only way for SXSW to save itself at this point is for it to shrink radically, which won't happen – it brings in too much money, and for better or worse, still draws huge crowds every year. No other festival even comes close, although plenty are trying. But at least if it shrunk, and pivoted a bit, it might have a point again.

Why are people even going to SXSW anymore? No one "discovers" bands there – that's what we have the internet for. No one gets deals done there because no one ever makes it to their meetings. Tech startups all chat with one another, but they can do that in the Bay Area and New York all the time anyway. Again, bands and beer equals fun, sure, but then it's just like Coachella or ACL or Bonnaroo, just more spread out.

It won't happen next year, or even ten years from now, but eventually SXSW will implode and have to start anew. It's a shame it got to the point where it's at now, but if nothing else, it might provide a valuable lesson to other music and tech upstarts – focus on growing smarter, not faster.

## Broken Windows

Twitter went nuts late Sunday night with the "early" release of the highly anticipated and legitimately excellent new Kendrick Lamar record. A few hours after it happened, the album briefly disappeared from iTunes while remaining live on Spotify; a few more hours after that it was back on sale. A source told me that Spotify was supposed to have the exclusive and launch a week early, and that iTunes jumped the gun (they didn't specify whether this was an honest mistake on Apple's part, or something more sinister).

This weird little kerfuffle shows us that windowing is still alive and well, despite its obvious limitations and the fact it presents a major disadvantage for consumers. In an era when the guiding media philosophy of most people seems to be "consumption on demand and without apology," making listeners jump through hoops is a terrible strategy. People love to bring up the straw-woman Taylor Swift argument here; first, she's a massive superstar in the top 1% of artists and an exception, not a rule, and second, she probably did lose listeners by only releasing her album in certain formats. Whether she cares or not is another matter.

It has been argued that windowing will save the music business, because it seems to be working for film and TV. There are a couple big holes in that argument, and I'll address them right after I finish watching this show on Popcorn Time.

First, there is enough different content on each platform that it makes sense to subscribe to both Netflix and Hulu (I'm leaving Amazon Prime about because it's part of a much larger program, and seems more like an add-on than a standalone product). The problem with applying this theory to streaming music sites is that the sites have the exact same content most of the time, and many hours of prestige TV or several seasons of a sitcom just aren't the same as the small handful of albums that people care about enough make windowing them worthwhile. The level of urgency involved in listening to music is different than TV, as well – there are no spoilers on albums. You might be excited to listen to something, but it's not going to change your experience that much if a bunch of people on social media say a record is great, or awful, or somewhere in the middle. If I miss Mad Men on Sunday night, I avoid Twitter until I've seen the latest episode; I can't imagine anyone staying offline until they've had a chance to hear an album.

The second argument people trot out pertains to movies, and the fact that people are still going to theaters to see films when they first come out – a hurdle much greater than simply signing up for another music service. There are a few holes in this argument – first, there is no way to see a first run movie unless it is in the theaters, unless you want to hunt down a bootleg DVD and have a far inferior viewing experience. A torrented album generally has pretty much the same sound quality as the same record on iTunes or Spotify; a weird shaky video shot from the back of a theater is almost always awful.

Going to the movies is still seen as a social experience, for reasons I honestly can't fathom. I'll veer off into my personal opinion here, which is that seeing a movie in a theater is a terrible user experience, and I'm still shocked no one has disrupted it. I wanted to go see Chappie over the weekend, but none of the three times it was being shown at my local cinema worked for me, so I wound up staying home. I would have happily given the filmmakers money to watch it on my own time, but the movie business has yet to figure out just how much money they are leaving on the table.

Back to music, and the fact that we need to end the exclusivity arms race before it kills us all. This seems to be a ghastly hangover of the big box era CD retailing era, when every store wanted a slightly different version of a release, so that people would buy it at Walmart and not Target, or what have you. I've never seen anyone argue that one different track made someone decide to purchase a CD along with detergent or whatever they happened to be buying, but somehow the notion that exclusivity was desirable has stuck around. There was also no upfront cost to the consumer if somehow the extra Britney Spears remix was worth waiting to buy it at another store – maybe a few bucks of gas money, but nothing like signing up for an app, starting a new membership, and paying a bill every month.

Here's the real reason windowing needs to die – rationing content in the age of plenty makes no sense. I've argued for the death of the album format on many occasions and will continue to do so; the biggest celebs with the teen crowd are YouTube stars who release content daily, and expecting kids to wait an entire album cycle, then have to take even more action to hear an album is just dumb. Put it on one streaming site and it'll be on torrents in an hour. Put it everywhere and at least you'll be able to monetize it.

If streaming services really want to continue with exclusives, they should go the full Netflix and start signing artists directly. That at least makes some financial sense, and they would have the option to license out the release to other outlets if they wanted to. I'm baffled that no streaming services have launched sub-labels, given the incredible success of original programming on sites like Netflix. I can only speculate they have non-compete clauses in their label deals, and when it comes time to renegotiate, they push back.

There are so many other things streaming services can do to set themselves apart from one another – price being the biggest, but great design, fantastic playlists and other features, and ease of use are all key. To coerce people into signing up because they're holding an anticipated record hostage feels lazy at best and disingenuous at worst.

## Why Are Recommendations So Incomplete?

Most people agree that the days of the mass cultural phenomenon are probably over. One in five American households are never going to watch the same thing, as they did with the Motown 25 concert. There will still be huge bands, but they'll be huge within a particular crowd – teen pop bands, country superstars, etc. Every so often there will be a blockbuster film, like Avatar, but even those are rare – and compared to something like Titanic, which it seems like everyone saw, plenty of people skip the big hits every summer and come through just fine.

Instead, we are sectioning ourselves off into smaller and smaller niches, and everything we consume within those niches tends to align. Hipster Harriet likes prestige TV dramas, indie rock, mumblecore films, eating vegan or paleo, and dense novels that grace the cover of the Times book review. Redneck Rosie likes Duck Dynasty, country music, blockbuster comedies, fast food, and books that appear on the Times bestseller list.

Obviously, this is super reductive, and plenty of people like a big mix of things outside what they'd be expected to like based on income, location, and education. But take a look at yourself, and you'll probably see that more often than not, your consumption patterns tend to align in a very particular way.

Which is why I'm honestly shocked that no one in the entertainment space seems to have figured this out. When I went on iTunes to buy a few TV shows to watch on the plane ride home from SXSW, the site was totally siloed into film, TV, and music sections – with no recommendations based on what I liked or purchased in other parts of the site. I'll say upfront that I'm not a huge iTunes user, so the information could have been incomplete – but regardless, iTunes still has my credit card info and my address, and they could at least glean something from that. A Williamsburg zip code should be a pretty dead giveaway about my potential preferences.

It's not just Apple – Amazon fails at this, too. Their recommendations within categories are usually solid, but they've never recommended something in a different category based on an order. I ordered Kim Gordon's memoir and it didn't even take the obvious step of recommending Sonic Youth albums. I dug around and the only site I could find that offered cross-platform recommendations required you to enter them manually, and was woefully incomplete – when I entered Karl Ove Knausgaard, the site had "never heard of him;" entering TV on the Radio got me a whopping two book recommendations, both by well-known authors.

I connect my Spotify account to my Facebook page and I've never had them recommend anything based on any of the content they could possibly glean from it. And I'm not even talking about the deeper stuff they could pull – for instance, that I loved a recent episode of the The Americans that featured a Fleetwood Mac sync, and that it might be a good time to revisit "Rumours." I'm talking about really simple things, like "you liked the Kurt Cobain documentary, how about listening to Nirvana?"

What I find galling is not that I have so much information about myself on the web – I put it all out there – but that no one can use it in any meaningful, smart way to serve me good content. My Facebook page says that I like doing crossfit, distance running, and eating clean; perhaps serve me with some great workout playlists (and don't serve me ads for juice boxes, good lord). Facebook's ad algorithms are clunky as hell, as well as being straight out of the 1950's – as soon as I got engaged I got wedding ads, once I changed my status to married, here came the baby ads – and I'm surprised they can't figure out something better.

Which leads me back to Amazon and Apple, and how they could use this as a real way to set themselves apart and win the streaming wars. As much as I like Netflix, they don't have access to music; Spotify only has music, no movies or TV. But Amazon has everything, and they know everything. My doorman probably hates my guts because he signs for five Prime packages for me every day. Amazon knows where I live, what shoes I buy, and what my dog eats – and they can't figure out how to put that together and recommend me some new music.

I do remember Target doing this with circulars a while back and catching flack for outing a pregnant teenager based on her purchase history, and maybe the recommendations I'm seeing are just so sneaky and under the radar that I'm missing them. I kind of doubt it, though – my guess is that companies just haven't figured out how all the pieces fit when it comes to recommending culture. But there's really no downside to giving it a try – no one will stop using Apple or Amazon if they recommend some books or films they don't like. In fact, they'll probably offer feedback that will help improve future recommendations.

And this is where Apple and iTunes and whatever Beats becomes can really kick ass. Apple doesn't have as much as Amazon, because they don't sell as much as Amazon, but they have enough in terms of credit card info and film, TV, and music consumption. I'd love to log in and see my whole cultural footprint reflected in the content I'm being served.

A lot of people I've interviewed have complained that streaming services are too focused on genre, when they really like multiple types of music that fit a particular mood or experience. Hopefully, by taking into account other things that people consume and learning how they all fit together, a company could provide recommendations that reflect a bigger picture.

## Tidal Wave or Shallow Puddle?

Will Jay-Z's new streaming service deliver real change – or just more of the same?

**What is Tidal?** If you cared enough to read this piece, you probably know that Tidal is the streaming music service, owned by Jay-Z and a number of other high profile artists, that "relaunched" today with a splashy press conference. Jay bought Tidal's parent company, Swedish music streaming company Aspiro, earlier this year – Tidal has technically been live since the fall of last year, but the promotions today are supposed to officially launch the site.

Tidal has a few selling points – the service offers two tiers, a $9.99/month tier that looks like pretty much every other streaming service, and a $19.99 tier that features high quality audio. Deezer tried something similar with "Deezer Elite" for its US launch last year – and how many Deezer Elite users have you met in your travels?

Then, there are promises of exclusives, which make sense given all the high profile artists involved with the service. The only problem is that, as I've discussed before, exclusives aren't all that valuable in the music world. Artificial scarcity in a world of unlimited content makes no sense and all. If Tidal can hoard content such that it becomes the only place to go in order to hear the vast majority of high profile artists, it has a shot, but that would mean defeating a number of streaming services already in the market. Tidal has exclusive concert videos from a handful of artists, as well as a playlist Beyonce made, but I don't know if that's worth it for many people.

## Is Tidal all the different from (Spotify, Rdio, Beats)?

At this point, not really. The desktop site does include high quality official video, which is nice, but it wasn't such a challenge to open up a YouTube window if you really wanted to watch a video. Otherwise, it's more of the same – a bunch of playlists, new releases, and searchable catalogs. It seems as complete as all the other services. The user experience is fine. If you've used any other streaming service, you know what to expect.

I don't think Tidal is trying to steal customers from Spotify etc. The market of people who have never used a streaming service is still massive, and up for grabs. One thing Tidal doesn't have is a radio function, which puts it at a significant disadvantage when it comes to pulling in casual users who just want a lean-back, Pandora-style experience.

Tidal also supposedly pays more and is "artist-owned," although the artist owners in question are people like Madonna and Kanye West. Given the lack of ads and free tier (although they are offering 30 day free trials), scaling up to the point where they can pay artists substantially more than other services might be difficult.

One of the selling points is that Tidal is "artist-friendly," but as plenty of people have pointed out, if the average person cared all that much about artist royalties, Napster never would have happened.

One of the most interesting potential differentiators is addressed in a Billboard interview with Jay-Z

**"So, Tidal launches today. Creatively, what do you hope happens, beginning tomorrow?**

Artists come here and start making songs 18 minutes long, or whatever. I know this is going to sound crazy, but maybe they start attempting to make a "Like a Rolling Stone," you know, a song that doesn't have a recognizable hook, but is still considered one of the greatest songs of all time, the freedom that this platform will allow art to flourish here. And we're encouraging people to put it in any format they like. It doesn't have to be three minutes and 30 seconds. What if it's a minute and 17, what if it's 11; you know, just break format. What if it's just four minutes of just music and then you start rapping?"

I was actually planning on an April Fools prank where I broke the news that Spotify was buying Soundcloud, but this could be just as good. One thing that no streaming service has done is work with unofficial content, be it songs that an artist threw together in a studio and wants to release right away or remixes or anything of that nature. If Tidal can work with artists to release music that doesn't fit the normal release format, that might be a massive selling point.

**Should we believe the hype?**

Look, we were all weirded out by that press conference. I saw Lady Gaga play piano at the Vevo party and got drunk at the Beyond Oblivion shindig – a great launch with tons of famous people does not a great product make. The product as it is now is decent, but not great. Having Kanye tweet about something gets you about a week of attention, if that.

In a way, Tidal is a product without an audience. Hardcore fans probably already use Spotify or Rdio and there's not much to convince them to shift. Casual fans are using Pandora for background music. Older fans are probably beyond the point of signing up for something because someone famous promoted it. Younger fans weren't really represented on stage, except by Nicki Minaj and Rihanna. Rock fans only got Arcade Fire (BTW, Win, please square your comments about broke artists "selling out" by accepting free burritos with your decision to own part of a streaming company) and Jack White, who now has interests in both vinyl pressing and streaming music. He's the music version of the corporate exec who gives money to both parties, just to be sure.

The one big question is whether all the competition in the market will ever drive down prices. Apple wasn't about to get to a cheaper tier for the Beats launch, and no one has cracked the $9.99 price point. By having a free tier, Spotify is still in a stronger position.

**So, get it or skip it?**

By all means, get the free trial and give it a go. If you're a real super audiophile, it might be worth it. Otherwise...I'd wait to see what Beats does and make a decision then.

**Is Bundling How We Finally Get People to Pay for Music?**

If you're anything like me, you've spent the last week reading through the cascade of snark raining down on Tidal. Once you cut away jokes about Jay-Z and the Illuminati, the consensus seems to be that the service is fine – it's just pointless. It has albums, and playlists, and "exclusives," (which all show up on YouTube within minutes of being posted), but nothing about it seems all that compelling.

Then again, for average users, nothing about any of these services seems all the compelling, at least in the sense that they are not opening their wallets to pay for them. I've been talking to non-music-business friends about Tidal for the Upward Spiral podcast, and most of them don't even pay for music. They use the free tiers of Pandora and Spotify, and YouTube, and Songza. When I asked one of them what would compel her to pay for music, she replied "if it was part of Netflix, just another drop-down option on the menu."

So what if it's that simple? What if, instead of a streaming service being the "Netflix for music," it was "Netflix and music?" All your entertainment content, all in one place, for a flat fee every month. Of all the people I talk to about not paying for music streaming, they all pay for Netflix, Hulu, or Amazon Prime.

There are a several reasons people are willing to pay for film and TV but not music. The "free options" for film and TV have never been great, and downloading films and TV shows from torrent sites has always been trickier technically than downloading music. Hulu offers a handful of free shows, but everything else lives behind a paywall – and as everyone who has a cable bill knows, even watching TV on an actual TV isn't free. The content available on YouTube doesn't generally have the same production quality as a film or TV – and while there are some great viral videos and webisodes out there, the producers of Games of Thrones aren't exactly worried.

There are legions of free and decent sources for music – the aforementioned free tiers of Spotify and Pandora, 8tracks and Songza,

YouTube and Soundcloud. Piracy has dropped in recent years as more alternatives have launched – but converting people from pirate to paying is hard, especially when there are good free alternatives in the middle.

Watching films and TV is also, for the most part, a lean-forward experience – when you're watching TV, you're either fully invested or using second screens in a secondary capacity (tweeting about the show during commercial breaks, for instance). Music, on the other hand, is now a lean-back experience, even if you're consciously selecting tracks or making playlists. Music is an "in-addition;" you're listening and chatting with friends, or running, or working.

So it would make total sense that music live in a service with other streaming entertainment. It has been tried before – Rdio launched Vdio, a film and TV site, in 2013, but the service never made it out of beta and died after six months. It's early death can be traced to Rdio's low overall numbers and the fact that the service mirrored the current iteration of iTunes more than Netflix; it was a pay as you go model with fairly high prices to rent films and TV shows.

Amazon Prime arguably does this now, but they very little effort into their streaming service. The catalog is limited, playlists seem to be curated by robots, and the overall user experience is clunky. Amazon certainly has the resources to build something better, but their attention seems to be focused elsewhere.

Which leaves two alternatives – Netflix merges with an existing player, or Apple goes in and burns everything down.

It makes perfect sense for the folks at Apple to break out the flamethrower. Right now, the iTunes experience is resoundingly average – it's pay as you go downloads and rentals for films and TV, which is still OK in certain situations (watching on airplanes, staying up to date on current shows), but still feels old-fashioned. The product is oddly chopped up, with everything siloed – but what if they built a really beautiful player where you could cruise around and have everything in one place? Love the Fleetwood Mac sync from the Americans earlier this season? Here, stream Rumours, or buy tickets to their next show.

Apple could set one price for everything – all the music, film, and TV you want, in one well-designed place, all the time. They'd win the day. It would kill all the other streaming services, all the other video services, and maybe even take out the cable companies while they're at it. This could be the end of Time Warner. Imagine that for a second. That ugly DVR box could be replaced by an Apple TV in every household in a few years.

Of course, Netflix and Spotify (or Tidal, or Deezer) could also merge and start something pretty excellent, especially if Apple drags their feet. And it wouldn't be the worst thing in the world to have a little competition, if only to help keep prices down and provide alternatives.

The real takeaway here is that throwing exclusives or hi-def audio at people isn't going to make them convert when there are so many good, free options out there. Plenty of folks at streaming music services have looked at Netflix's numbers and wondered why they couldn't come close, but that's the wrong question. They can't beat 'em – maybe they should join them.

## Paid Streaming's Real Enemy is YouTube

The biggest enemy for any paid streaming service (Tidal, Spotify, Rdio, Deezer, Beats, etc) is not another paid streaming service, or any of the non-interactive radio services like Pandora or Songza. It's YouTube. And unfortunately for streaming services and some players in the music industry, YouTube looks pretty unbeatable.

The most galling part is, YouTube doesn't seem to care that much about music. They pay lip service in interviews and have deals with artists to monetize plays based on ad revenues, but given that music accounts for around 40% of all content streamed on the site, it doesn't come across as being a high priority. YouTube's massive ad campaign on the New York City subway didn't mention music at all. Its paid service, YouTube Music Key, was launched with little fanfare last year and has languished in beta ever since.

While YouTube does pay rights holders, the rates are low. Music Ally analyzed an IFPI (International Federation of the Phonographic Industry) report and found that "the ARPU (average revenue per user) between the likes of Spotify at one end of the scale and YouTube at the other has never been more pronounced...YouTube users each contribute the equivalent of just one download purchase each a year to label income."

The average consumer, however, cares not one whit about this. They just want to listen to what they want, when they want, and YouTube provides that in spades. Albums that aren't available on streaming services are on YouTube – while I couldn't find the masterful Geraldine Fibbers album "Lost Somewhere Between the Earth and My Home" on any service, it was easy listen to on YouTube. Then of course, there are those Liverpudlian white whales of streaming, the Beatles. Not on Spotify, Tidal, or Rdio...but it took less than 20 seconds for me to pull up a playlist of their number one hits and listen away on YouTube.

YouTube is also the only place for most of the live and unofficial content fans want to see. About a year ago, a friend recommended I check out

Future Islands Letterman performance, so to YouTube I went. After I watched it, YouTube started serving me more of the band's videos, so I stayed. For anyone who comes to a band via a recommendation to check out a live clip, YouTube remains the only game in town. This is to say nothing of the hundreds of bedroom covers and remixes available on YouTube that can't be found anywhere else. The sheer volume of content on the site far surpasses anything other streaming services can offer.

Oh, and those "exclusives" other services are touting? Yup, they're all on YouTube within moments of being launched on other platforms – usually slightly sped up or slowed down to evade YouTube's Content ID system, but sounding pretty much the same as what you'd have to pay to hear.

The product is not great, but that's almost beside the point. Making playlists is a cumbersome process; the app doesn't allow offline caching of playlists (Music Key subscribers can pay for this); and the app doesn't run in the background so you can listen to music while doing other things on your phone. Annoying? Sure. But annoying enough to pay $120 per year to overcome?

As was referenced in the tweet at the top of the piece, kids love YouTube. They watch Minecraft tutorials and PewDiePie clips all day long. They watch shorts their friends make and clips of TV shows – and they mix music into this playlist. More than one person has suggested to me that people would pay for music if it was integrated into Netflix – and kids have created an oddly DIY version of this on YouTube. For them, it's all one big content stream.

There's also, I think, a shift in perception among younger kids. If you came of age in the eighties and nineties, you'll remember the "DIY revolution;" now, that idea has morphed and maybe even won out. Average looking people who talk about video games can become huge stars based on their personality and building a following – no agents or TV execs needed. Kids with guitars in bedrooms can amass huge online followings before labels pick them up – the gatekeepers are coming to the game later and later. The sense of "anyone can create something" has shapeshifted into "anyone, including me, can create something – but since the creators are people like me, they're not so special, after all."

Superstars will never go away, but fan expectations are different – they want another kind of interaction, one without as many hurdles. And YouTube, where they can consume it all, in one place, for free, provides that in a way official services just can't.

So does this mean streaming services should all just pack up and go home? No, but it does mean they need to take another look at their products. Allowing "unofficial" content on streaming services would be a great place to start, and as painful as it could be, lowering the price point might be a solution. Even though converting from free to anything is the hardest step to take, $3.99 for a better experience seems like an easier sell.

As it stands now, YouTube still reigns supreme, and the economics of that don't look good for the record business. They need to start doing something, fast, before YouTube crushes them completely.

## What Are Music Videos For, Anyway?

A small addendum to last week's YouTube piece: a few nights ago, a buddy of mine was liveblogging the South African Music Awards, and because I will killing some time until Mad Men came on, I decided to check out some of the winners. I know that South Africa is not a major music market, but it's not nothing, either, and these artists are big enough to be winning important awards. I fired up Spotify, and – nothing. No recommendations, either. So, to YouTube I went, and spent the next hour happily getting to know Beatenberg, who are great. Again, I'm fully aware that I'm one of the few people in the US who cared about this, but these artificial limits still make no sense.

Now, on to the broader question about audio-visual consumption – in the age of YouTube, Vine, and Meerkat/Periscope, what is a music video, anyway? And what value does it provide?

I like Empire a lot, but one of most dated moments on the show's last season came when Hakeem begged for three million dollars to make a music video, and was then shown enjoying all the tropes of hip-hop videos of yore – girls in a hot tub, jet skis, etc. First, there's no way a music video would cost three million dollars today unless someone just wanted to burn cash; and two, what exactly was the point of this video? Unless it was some sort of ironic wink-nod to the old videos that was intended to go viral, it probably would have fallen flat.

Right now, the traditional music video is weirdly both as important as it has ever been, and less important than it ever was. A good viral video can make, if not a career, at least a hit and a nice whack of cash. Remember Ok Go, Baauer, or Psy? At the same time, MTV hasn't driven the conversation in years, unless the conversation is about why you shouldn't have a baby at sixteen or trust your internet boyfriend. If you're a major artist, making a big video might not do much for your career; "Shake It Off" was fun and all, but people would have been talking about Taylor Swift anyway.

Making a viral video is an art, not a science, especially if you're a smaller artist. Kanye riding a motorcycle while being straddled by Kim Kardashian drew a lot of attention and some great parodies because everything those two do draws a lot of attention. There are lots of videos that had all the right ingredients to go viral but never took off for any number of reasons. Part of it is because you compete with a much larger set of content when you make a video – when someone says "listen to this song," it's only competing for your attention with other songs (and maybe podcasts or audiobooks). When someone says "watch this video," it competes for your eyes and ears with every other music video, TV clip, movie trailer, video of a kid making an insane half-court shot, etc.

You also have to take into account that a decent size chunk of your audience probably won't even watch the music video you put on YouTube – that's the audience that uses it as a streaming player. In which case, the plain old lyric video starts to look pretty good. Hell, you can just leave it to the fans to upload the tracks and add pictures of your album cover or their dog as visuals and call it a day. You cede control of the image and the conversation – the last thing you want is your heartfelt breakup track to rise to prominence because Buzzfeed liked the use of it as backing track to someone's cat album – but you also pay nothing. And while backdooring your way into a viral video isn't something you can really try to do, it might pay off if you handle it right.

Then we get to short attention span theater, AKA Vine and Instagram video. Are these even music videos? Done well, they can be – but they're still pushing up against a lot of self-imposed limits. I've written before about the need to broaden the definition of a song; maybe a cool chorus or snappy sample is really all people want, in which case, a clever 15-second video makes sense. More problematic is that Vine and Instagram are both walled off by their owners, and people still don't think of them as places to see "music videos." This will change as people get more creative, but until there are a few big shifts, they'll remain far behind.

And finally, we come to Meerkat and Periscope. If you've been to a certain type of concert in the last few months, you've had the "pleasure" of watching the concert through someone's phone as they used the app to livestream it. Meerkat and Periscope exist in a weird legal grey area, the same area that has choked the life out of live streaming startup after live streaming startup. Unless you want to alienate your audience by banning phones, you're kind of stuck with this as the new normal. On any given evening you can search for shows at mid-sized indie venues and stumble across a few streams of varying quality.

It in no way competes with the live experience. It can induce FOMO in your friends who blew off the show, and it can provide a nice thumbnail for people considering buying tickets to a future show. It can also expose bad shows and hold artists who slack through their sets accountable, which is always a good thing. The one thing you can't do is use these apps to premiere old school music videos, as we saw with Madonna's disastrous Meerkat experiment. Meerkat is not a place where you show a music video; a Meerkat stream is the music video.

The old format video, such as it is, remains king, but the new kids are coming up from behind. Is there a future without the three-minute, highly produced clip on the horizon? Not anytime soon – but don't count the other formats out.

## Music Startups and the Passion Problem

Ask almost any music startup founder why they started their company, and you're likely to hear a variation of the following: "I love music! I'm such a passionate fan and music changed my life."

Which, on one level, is fine. Music is great! Doing work in an area you're passionate about is awesome. But that passion can also be a double-edged sword, leading you to think that everyone is just as passionate as you are about a certain subject, and clouding your judgement about whether your product is actually something that can scale.

A few months back, Google User Experience Researcher Tomer Sharon posted a fantastic talk about perfectly executing the wrong plan. His presentation wasn't specifically aimed at music startups, but much of it rang true to me. As someone who has been to countless music hack days and demo events, as well as consulted and worked for several music startups, the six problems he outlined mapped perfectly onto many of failed startups I've seen.

The first problem is that creators assume their personal pains translated to something that the wider world actually needed. Now, sometimes this works – the founders of Uber probably noticed you couldn't get a cab in San Francisco and decided that was a pain point that needed to be addressed. But in music, that's not often the case – just because you want a fun way to share playlists with friends, it certainly doesn't mean everyone does. The truth is that most people just don't care that much about music as you do. Most people are happy to buy a few albums a year, maybe check out a few concerts, and listen to the radio in the car. That's hard for intense music fans to fathom sometimes, but it's the truth.

Unfortunately, if you surround yourself with other music fans, you're not likely to see this. The second problem is that startup founders often seek feedback from friends and family, who are likely to be biased. It stands to reason that if music is a big part of your life, you'll be drawn to people who also love music, and are likely to think your music startup idea is a great one. As for asking the non-music fans in your life, they're also unlikely to be brutally honest – your dad might not have bought an album since the eighties, but he's not going to be negative about your idea, either.

But, even after all that, let's say you go ahead and build your music startup. You put something together, you test it with users, and the users liked it – but it still never took off. Alas, fatal flaw number three – listening to users rather than observing their behavior.

Concert subscription startup Jukely raised $8 million this week, and good on them. They are joining a crowded market, and I fear that they are going to fall prey to the same fallacies that have plagued other live music startups. It's not the concerts aren't easy to find; it's that they are not easy to attend for many people. The live music audience, for the most part, is made up of people in their twenties – mostly because people in their twenties in major cities can afford to go to shows and stay out late. They're just competing for the same small piece of the pie as everyone else, without addressing a bigger problem – concerts are off limits for people older than thirty, for the most part. The real problem for many people is not that they don't want to see music, it's that they can't stay out until midnight when they have careers and kids to think about. Rather than innovating around that problem, most concert startups simply write off older audiences and assume that only young people want to see music and just need new ways to access it.

This leads into the fourth problem, which is that most music startups don't test their riskiest assumption. That assumption, for many startups, is that no one really cares about music all that much. Spotify, Tidal, etc all operate from the assumption that enough people will care about music to pay $120 a year (or more) to listen – and that might not be the case. Even at the height of the boom in the late nineties, the average consumer spent about $28 a year on recorded music, and that was without all the free options available today.

The other risk startups take when entering the music space is that they simply don't know anything about the music business. The "launch first, ask questions later" mentality is hard to pull off in music – love it or hate it, the rights holders still call shots. And trust me, they're reading Techcrunch – if you launch a music startup without deals in place and raise a big round, prepare to kiss most of that money goodbye.

But by this point, founders are buried deep in problem five – the Bob the Builder mentality. They're lost sight of if they should build something and become totally focused on whether they can build something. I should point out here that I'm not opposed to building things are learning exercises; if you want to come to a Music Hack Day and build the ten millionth playlist sharing app just to learn how to manipulate a certain piece of code, go for it. Just don't try to go raise money for it.

Because here's what will happen: you will have perfectly executed the wrong plan. You'll have a sexy, cool music app that no one wants, needs, or cares about. The music tech business is a graveyard littered with startups that seemed so cool at the time, because the founders loved them. And maybe those founders found some people with money who thought that working in a bank was boring and investing in a music startup would be a great way to meet famous people and get dates. They all went to SXSW, and lit some money on fire, and crashed and burned a few years later.

And look, no one dies when this happens. The money goes to money heaven and everyone just goes and does something else. But the problem with building startups because you just love music and assume everyone else does is that you don't come any closer to solving the real problems. There are interesting businesses to be built in the music space; you just have to come at them from a colder, more analytical perspective. Passion is great, but in the end, it often fades.

# Do The Olds Hate Music, Or Does Music Hate the Olds?

I turn 35 today, which means I should be just about done with discovering new music and getting ready to crawl back under a sonic blanket of grunge and riot grrl for the remainder of my listening life. While that actually sounds kind of good, and I'll admit that most of the new music I like (Torres, Speedy Ortiz) is pretty similar to the old stuff I liked (PJ Harvey, Liz Phair), I'm still dutifully hitting Spotify each week to check out the new goods. According to their data scientists, though, I'm a unicorn.

But try taking my first sentence and subbing in any other form of culture for music. Would anyone ever argue that there's an age limit on discovering new TV, or film, or books, or visual art? How come, of all the forms of culture we consume, only music seems to have an age limit?

One of the arguments you hear a lot is that music is a visceral, powerful experience for teens and young adults, and that our response to music changes as we get older. Which makes sense, on one level; as Chuck Klosterman wrote in "Fargo Rock City," "I'll never love a band like that again because I'll never be fifteen again." When you're a self-centered kid with blazing hormones, every song seems to speak directly to you – mom and dad don't understand you! Popular kids are lame! You'll never get over your first love! As you mature and things calm down, you probably come back around to liking or at least respecting your folks, and you don't need Nine Inch Nails or Linkin Park to get you through the tough times.

But that doesn't mean new music can't hit you in an emotional way at any age. I played the new Sufjan Stevens album for my 70-year-old dad and he was deeply moved by it. I'm not only constantly hearing new stuff, but hearing it in different ways – Liz Phair's "Exile in Guyville" was a great album when I was thirteen, but I relate to it in a totally different way at thirty-five.

Enough anecdata, and back to the question – why does this only seem to happen in music?

For one, the whole production model is a little different, although film is starting to skew this direction. Think of it this way – unless an artist is a true visionary, all the albums they make over the course of a career will sound roughly the same. That's not a bad thing, it's just the way it is – artists and bands generally don't radically cross genres. They might experiment, but a rock band is not going to suddenly pivot to EDM overnight. Film does this a little with sequels and prequels and series, but it's rare that you'll get a solid version of the same series with the same cast every two years, while that's totally plausible in music. It's much easier to stick with certain bands for a lifetime because many of them will put out new music and continue to tour, and you don't need to do any more work. You can feel like you're discovering something new, because you're listening to a new album, even though it probably sounds a lot like all the old albums.

The engagement metrics around music are different as well. Film and TV and books are easier to measure – did you watch it (or read it) or not? Music is a little squishier. I've never consciously listened to a Meghan Trainor song, because I don't hate myself, but I've heard it at the drugstore and in commercials. Did I engage with it? Technically, yes, but not really. Did I discover it, in the sense that I know it exists? Yes, but I'll probably never interact with it on any other level. Because music is so ephemeral now, we're probably constantly hearing new stuff; we're just not retaining any of it.

Then we come to marketing, which I've been banging my drum about for a while. Most (though not all) new music marketing skews toward twenty-somethings and teens. There's a reason car ads for the olds feature classic rock and car ads for the kids feature fun. Aside from artists like Adele, who seem to transcend age-groups, there's a line – new pop for the kids, throwbacks and "old people music" for the others. Concerts are marketed almost entirely to young people unless they are reunion tours or the occasional classy festival. A huge part of the reason people in their thirties and up stop interacting with new music is that the music and touring industry make it very hard to interact with it.

Which is kind of silly, because older people tend to have more money, and are old enough to remember the days when music wasn't just free-flowing free information. We will buy your stuff! We might not buy t-shirts, because we have to wear grown-up clothes to work, but we'll buy the shit out of a classy silk screen on an album cover we can frame. We'll pay extra to see a show at a reasonable hour in a nice venue. Our money is yours for the taking, music business, if you'd look up from chasing the next big thing for five minutes.

Maybe we also need to revisit the metrics around what counts as music consumption. Going out to a concert is a much bigger ask than watching a TV show or a movie or reading a book, with the added negative that concerts generally only happen once or twice in each city, between certain hours. Maybe consumption is watching a live stream of a show, or passing an album onto a friend, or putting it on at a dinner party. Make consuming new music easier, and people of all ages will likely take you up on it.

# Why Killing Freemium is the Worst Thing For Artists

Last week, reports started to surface that Apple was trying to convince labels to "kill" Spotify's free tier, presumably by renegotiating when their current contracts expire. From a business perspective, this makes sense – when Apple launches its streaming service, it will offer a free trial but not a free tier, and will charge the same as Spotify and other streaming players in the market. As we've seen from the Tidal fiasco, offering exclusives doesn't get you very far, so aside from an established brand name and a user base who might forget to cancel one their free trial is up, Apple doesn't have much to differentiate itself.

Even if Spotify's free tier went away, we'd all still have YouTube. Apple would have a victory, but it would be a pretty Pyrrhic one – they'd just be sending people away from streaming as a concept. But now there are rumors that Apple is trying to get labels to pull content from YouTube, which could lead to YouTube putting its music content behind a paywall – and that would be a huge mistake. Sony has also pulled its content from Soundcloud, and the clock is ticking on it being able to sign deals with the majors. If YouTube started charging to access the site and Soundcloud disappeared, the world could become a far less friendly place for emerging artists.

None of this is new, of course. Streaming may be a new format but the concept of killing off free is much older – as anyone who lived through the eighties and remembers the "Home Taping is Killing Music" campaigns can attest. This campaign was then summarily mocked by a number of indie bands, for good reason – they were the ones who stood to benefit the most from those homemade tapes being passed around. That was music discovery before we had apps for it, kids.

Killing freemium is quite possibly the most artist-unfriendly move that can be made. Now, a group of artists will start shouting about devaluing music and wanting to be paid more, and I get that. But take another step back and think about who those artists are, and what they look like. Have you ever heard an emerging artist, or an artist from an emerging market, yell about freemium? What do David Lowery, Father John Misty, Thom Yorke, and David Byrne have in common? You can figure it out.

I'm not saying artists from emerging economies shouldn't demand fair pay or be willing to accept less; what I am saying is that we need to be realistic about what people will pay for and how they'll access it. Case in point – a buddy of mine live tweeted an award show in South Africa last month, and I wanted to check out some of the winners. Because Spotify hasn't launched in South Africa yet, their content from that market is limited, so onto YouTube I went. And guess what – some of the bands were great, and if they ever tour in the US, I'll probably go see them. If their labels look at viewer data, they'll likely see a small uptick in US viewership, and hopefully make something happen.

Or take the example of Psy (go back to 2012. I'll wait). Is that a sales pitch anyone would have initially bought? He's a chubby guy who sings in Korean and has a special dance. Not exactly an obvious chartbuster. But because it cost nothing, save a few minutes of time, to check out this weirdness, it grew like crazy. You think Baauer would have the hit he had if it wasn't for the virality of the Harlem Shake? On any given day, I can go down a rabbit hole of remixes of Australian tracks by an Indian DJ, or watch KPop videos until I think I'm going to have a seizure.

Do we really want to go back to an era when a small group of players controlled what most of us heard, and the only way to hear outsider artists was to trade tapes and mix CDs. And now we have easy ways to get free music, for which artists get paid nothing, and that will become the new normal for discovery? There are plenty of artists who credit Napster with helping them build their careers – but wouldn't it be better for artists to have something, rather than nothing.

As long as free options exist that aren't that much worse than the paid options, rational humans will choose the free one. And if big labels can erase Spotify's free option, what else can they do? They all have equity in Spotify as well, so they've hedged their bets and get paid either way – but what about the artists? And what about the artists who don't have label deals, or access to legit licensing deals? Should they just stay in their own backyard?

Look, there are lots of people out there who would love to get in a time machine and go back to 1999 – but think about all the people who lost out on that wealth. There were probably hundreds of artists in Lagos and Shanghai and Buenos Aires who were making amazing music but had no way to get it to anyone, or make any money off of it. Now, even in an imperfect system, they can still compete with established Western artists for the ears of consumers.

Killing freemium won't make people magically pay $9.99 a month; it'll make them seek out free music elsewhere. By blocking channels like YouTube and Soundcloud, the labels are sending a message that only music they approve of and want to monetize can be heard, and the door slams shut for many outsider artists. The last thing listeners want is a protectionist culture around the music they consume – every artist deserves a fair shot at being heard.

## No One Wants The Firehose

Remember how exciting we thought it was that we had all the world's information at our fingertips? Pages of search results! Millions of tracks! More hot takes than you could read in a lifetime! Now, it all just seems like too much. Twitter, the quintessential firehose of information, is planning on rolling out a new product that allows users to follow events rather than people – a way of narrowing the flow, albeit only slightly. Any major event, from the NBA playoffs to the horrific shooting in Charleston, will result in tons of often-repetitive posts. But it cuts of the jarring effect you see when you read five tweets about mass murder and then one about a funny cat.

This trend isn't just limited to Twitter. A few days ago, Wired ran a piece called "Apple and Google Race to See Who Can Kill the App First." With the launch of the Apple News feature, Apple effectively took out several new aggregation apps that were doing a fine job serving up content already – and heralded the beginning of the end of the information firehose. Pulse and Flipboard were both useful and widely used, but Apple News will come built in – a game changer. Now you can customize your news to suit exactly your tastes – no more digging through a newspaper or magazine (or their corresponding app) to find what you want to read.

Towards the end of the Wired piece, author John Pavlus wrote this: "But when it comes down to it, mobile users aren't interested [whether something is an app or a service]. We're more like the no-nonsense cartel kingpin in Miami Vice who coldly informs Crockett and Tubbs that "in this business, I do not buy a service. I buy a result."

Me, too. I don't want Yelp; I want to know where to eat. I don't care about Google Calendar; I care about not missing appointments. I don't buy iPhones; I buy best-in-class pictures of my kids. I'm loyal only to results, and I suspect you are, too."

Exactly. While I like the New York Times, it wouldn't be hard to me to read another news source that has better reporting on a topic I care about. I've been happy with Spotify, but I'll probably make the switch to Apple Music once it launches – and if, say, Google rolls out a better product in a few years, I won't think twice about moving over there.

Much of this has to do with the fact that most apps are totally de-personalized. I'd feel a little bad about not shopping at my local mom-and-pop if a megastore launched down the block, because I have some connection to the place in the form of a relationship with the owners. But it's pretty rare to be connected to a team behind an app – and even if you are, there's a decent chance that they'll fold, or pivot, or just move on. Deleting an app is shockingly easy to do.

The other issue is that most apps just feel overwhelming. I don't want a list of fifty places to eat, like Yelp gives me – I want one place that I know I'll like, that I can afford, and that has a table for two in forty-five minutes. I recently needed to get my air conditioner serviced and tried some of the major home repair sites, and came away with nothing but a list of numbers I had to call myself. What's the point of that? I want the best HVAC repair person at my door, today. A list of options is useless.

Some music services, to their credit, seem to learning and moving ahead of this. Spotify offers a number of contextual playlists, as does Songza; Spring offers playlists based on speed for athletes. But even that can be overwhelming – I just opened Spotify to find almost forty playlist tiles on the front page – and countless other tiles when I made my first choice. If I want to chill, do I want indie chill, rock chill, acoustic chill...? I don't know. All I know is I don't feel so chill anymore.

I interviewed a woman a while back about Tidal, and at one point asked her what her ideal music service would look like. She answered, "a big play button that I would tap once, and it would play me the exact right song."

This is probably impossible, but if we start moving towards a world where all our apps can talk to each other, maybe it's not as crazy as it seems. If my Apple News can tell that I've read ten stories about something depressing, maybe Apple Music serves me something happy to perk me up. If my socials are eventually absorbed into the background, perhaps it scans my posts and sees that I posted about an upcoming trip, and plays me music from that region. Or if I post about a movie I enjoyed, as I did last night, it could serve me music from that film.

There are plenty of downsides to all this close personalization. If I'm only being served things I'm likely to enjoy, I might get stuck in a comfort zone and miss out on learning opportunities. If an otherwise great track never seems like a perfect fit for my current mood, I'm unlikely to hear it. There is something to be said for taking a chance to a track, or a random film on Netflix, or reading an article on an unfamiliar topic.

But the firehose is already slowing to a stream, and as services and apps get smarter and communicate better, a manageable trickle. If music services take the hint and focus on the exact right song for the exact right moment, they're likely to encourage users to stick around – and come out ahead.

# Want Millennials to Start Paying for Music? Start Paying Them.

The DIY revolution has begun to devour its children.

If you immediately understood the above as nod to an oft-quoted Pat Buchanan line in the nineties culture wars, then you'll probably also remember the rise of the DIY movement. Anyone could start a band (hell, you didn't even need to know how to play an instrument). Your neighbor's garage band was just as good as whatever major label sellout was headlining the club that night – maybe even better, because they still had integrity, man. Rock stars weren't Gods but mere mortals to happened to have slightly better hair and the same neurosis. Eddie Vedder spent more time polishing his "aw, shucks, I'm a regular dude" persona than your average politician.

After some fits and starts, the movement seems to have taken hold and stuck. Part of that is due to the fact that it's easier than ever to record and share music – you can download a few cheap programs like AudioTool and Magix Music Maker, record some tracks, and post them on SoundCloud from wherever you are in the world. You don't have to be part of a scene, and or have any support – a kid in a slum has the same chance of going viral as a kid in LA. On almost every level, this is great. Allowing more talented artists to share their music is always a good thing, even if it means having to wade through a lot of trash. Fans have more control in terms of helping artists rise to the top. Geography is no longer a limiting factor when it comes to sharing art.

But on the other hand – if anyone can do it, is making music really that special? If any kid in a basement anywhere in the world can share a track for free – why pay for it? Kids are creating content all day long and not getting paid a dime – that's the new normal.

Think of the biggest companies of the internet age and how little they create. Facebook is a platform – if we didn't spend hours uploading photos and sharing Buzzfeed quizzes and arguing with out uncles about gun control, it would just be a bunch of code. We are the ones who keep

Facebook going – and yet I've never been paid for my "work." Ditto for Twitter. And Instagram. And Snapchat. And Vine.

Millennials spend hours and money on this stuff, and most of them never see a dime. Even if they do, chances are they're not being paid by Twitter or Snapchat – they're being paid by brands in order to access their followers. And the vast majority never get that far – they're just creating stuff to share with friends or to broadcast their thoughts. By breaking down most of the barriers to entry when it comes to sharing creativity, we've also broken down the mystique that you need to somehow be "special" to be a creator.

All this propping up of Mark Zuckerberg and Jack Dorsey's empires aside, millennials are also the first generation that is expected to work for free. It's not enough to have a bunch of internships on your resume during college – now many millennials intern for free post-college, too. And they're also expected to build a social following and network outside of their eventual paid work, which they're almost never compensated for.

The move towards social has also prompted radical changes in consumption patterns. The argument I almost always get about millennials and their willingness to pay for music is that they are willing to pay for concert tickets, which in the case of big festivals can run into the hundreds of dollars. This is totally true, and here's why – you can Instagram a concert. Before the rise of social, the only people you could show off to were people in your immediate vicinity – so having a flashy car or huge record collection made sense. Now you can spread your images around the world – but taking a picture of a bunch of digital files is boring. A selfie backstage at Coachella has far more social currency.

Now we're at the stage where anybody can be anything, and almost everyone is doing a few things. Rappers are making hundreds of dollars driving Lyft between unpaid SXSW shows. Millennials are working at social media agencies during the day and then building their own Vine followings at night. No one is making that much money, anyway, and if they are it's probably being spent on experiences (and student loans).

One of the solutions to all this would be to pay people for their social labor, but that'll never happen. We all work the social second shift now, creating #personalbrands, and we're just expected to do that without seeing any return. There doesn't seem to be much interest in a worker-owned social platform.

The other problem is that now the veil has been lifted, it can't really come back down. Rock stars were never magic people – they were just good looking and talented, but not impossible to replicate. If it's just as good an experience to listen to your buddy's SoundCloud mixes, then some of the mystique is gone. If we're all in the same boat, we're all on the Titanic.

The new normal is likely lots of unpaid creation, with the best (or most popular) creations being bought by the highest bidder. That high bidder will probably be a brand, and that brand will continue to share the content for free while attaching their own messaging (and might even just recreate your content without paying you a dime). No one pays with money and we all pay with our eyeballs. Kids will never stop creating – they'll just find new ways to live, and make a living, while doing it.

## Apple Music is Finally Here – Should Spotify be Worried?

Pretty much everyone I know was updating to iOS 8.4 this morning – and it wasn't because they were psyched about iBooks improvements. Apple Music is finally alive and ready for use – but is it ready for primetime? And should Tidal, Spotify, and Pandora be worried?

After choosing a plan and accepting the terms and conditions, you wind up on a screen with many bouncing pink bubbles, just like the old Beats app. It's an odd choice, given that younger listeners seem to be trending away from thinking about music in genre categories, and the UX is also clunky – you're asked to interact with both genres you like and dislike. It also drives home what a walled garden Apple Music is – rather than asking to connect to your socials and seeing what you like, you have to make the effort to pick genres. Music fans like me are fine with this, but I can see this being frustrating for a casual listener.

Once you're finished with the bubbles, you're asked to pick three artists based on bubble choices. I was familiar with all the artists I picked, but I can definitely see cases where people would be frustrated if they didn't know some of the artists in the bubbles they were presented.

Mercifully, you're done with the bubbles after this, and get a selection of playlists "For You." I got a Japanese Fringe Rock playlist that I was pretty excited about, a Radiohead B-sides playlist that seems interesting, and a Flaming Lips playlist, as well as a bunch of album recommendations (Sonic Youth, Pixies, Liars). None of the albums were new, and a few were really old, making me think they're going to serve up musical comfort food rather than discovery in this section.

Click over to "New" and you'll see Taylor Swift's "1989" front and center; it's not technically a new record but it's a sweet middle finger to Spotify. The new music album selection doesn't seem curated at all and is just a bunch of new releases; scroll down even more to find "hot tracks;" why they qualify as hot is unclear. Then you get "recent releases" where I guess stuff that came out last week goes. Then "top songs;" unclear as to why these are "top" and not "hot."

Also, this is a lot of scrolling.

Then there's "Connect Video," which features video of a few artists talking to the camera, and "Connect Audio" which features some tracks, for some reason. Then playlists. Then music videos. Then hot albums, one of which is from last year and one of which is a best-of. Then more playlists. Then "new artists."

This is busy. It's overwhelming and just too many choices. When you click on the playlists, you can choose genres of activities, and then playlists within those genres and activities. All are credited to "Apple Music [genre]" which seems impersonal and robotic – I'd much rather know Susan, who is an expert in a certain type of music and also loves biking, is putting together my playlists. You can scroll through playlists forever and just keep getting more options. The curator section offers media outlet playlists, some of which make sense (Rolling Stone, Pitchfork) and some less so (Vogue, Wired).

Despite announcing that Beats1 would launch an hour after the app went live, I was able to listen to it as soon as I downloaded Apple Music – and was treated to an hour of ambient Brian Eno tracks with a snippet of Zane Lowe testing his mic. Those of us in the know figured this out pretty quickly and even had a few Twitter giggles – but think of the average listener. If I'm Joe-on-the-street who thinks Beats1 sounds neat and I get drone and mic checks out of the gate, it's not a great look. Given Apple's perfectionism, it also seems weird and sloppy that they didn't just launch everything at the same time or just toss up a decent playlist while we waited for Zane.

The one thing I noticed about the radio function, which has the potential to be killer, is that you can stream a few non-music channels as well. Right now I'm just seeing ESPN and WNYC, but I'd love more options, as well as the ability to listen to podcasts in the app. If Apple can make this the app where I go to listen to everything, that would be fantastic.

Finally, we get to Connect, which is a social network of sorts. I was served content from two of the artists I selected in the bubble game and got a live version of a Sonic Youth track and a video of FKA Twigs doing some choreography...OK. I tried to add other artists but wound up with an infinite loading circle. The lame Sonic Youth offering points to a larger problem – what to do with bands who aren't together anymore and can't produce viral content, or simply don't want to. And how to offer content that is compelling and not available anywhere else, without going in the direction of exclusive tracks or video that'll just wind up on YouTube five minutes later. Maybe an AmEx presale model for concert tickets in the app is an answer? Maybe the ability to chat with artists?

If you've been paying a shred of attention, you know that Apple Music was built by people who love music. Dr Dre, Jimmy Iovine, Trent Reznor, Ian Rogers, Dave Allen...all these guys have devoted their lives to making and promoting music. And that's awesome. And it's also Apple Music's biggest flaw.

This is an app for crate diggers. It's an app for people who want to scroll, dig deep, and put in some legwork. Personally, I really like it and can see myself using it – but I'm not sure about the silent majority. Apple has brought many things to the masses – it remains to be seen if streaming music is the next one.

## What Happens When Music Apps Die?

The column is going up a little late this week because I've spent the last few days up in Boston with my partner in podcasting, Kyle Bylin. We've been sitting in on and presenting at the Berklee Institute for Creative Entrepreneurship (ICE) Summer Camp for International High School Students, as well as drinking beer and spitballing about the future of the music business. We spent quite a bit of time chatting about apps, given that streaming music and other apps tend to be seen as the "future" of the music biz.

But as Panos Panay, who runs Berklee ICE, pointed out on a panel we did, apps are terrible. They're clunky, and there are too many of them, and they all only do one thing. I have my music app, and my yoga studio class booking app, and my app that I use to record my expenses, among many, many others. None of them communicate with each other. My music app can't look at the my maps app and serve me songs based on my destination. Kindle doesn't communicate with Netflix and suggest further reading based on documentaries I've watched. Instagram doesn't talk to Yelp to note where I'm taking pictures and suggest places to eat based on that location. And on and on.

I'm not the first person to complain about how siloed apps are, and I won't be the last. Already more and more apps are being baked into one another – Google Maps and Waze being a perfect example. It's not far-fetched to think that a few years down the road, Apple Music will incorporate data from my social feeds, my health feeds, and any other information I might provide it, and provide music curated just for me.

I'm still having conversations about Apple Music and hearing the same thing from most of the people I consider to be casual music fans – the service is too damn complicated. Sure, it provides you with a ton of curated options – but even sorting through the curated options can seem like a lot of work. One of the reasons people tell me they like Pandora is that it's pretty idiot-proof – type in the name of an artist and hit start.

Imagine if you didn't even have to do that. Imagine if your device just scanned every input, all the time, and delivered you music based on all that – and all you had to do was press the play button. It would basically be radio, except customized entirely for you. Obviously, some people would opt out of this due to privacy concerns and other issues – but given how much information we share freely right now, I think many people would just shrug and listen to music.

This is where we're going – but what exactly does it mean? For one, it means the death of many music apps, since we don't really need them. Why do we need a music discovery app when another entity can just do the discovering for us, and base it on the data versus guessing what we might like? If we can integrate our calendar function, it can tell us exactly when bands we like are coming to town – and if it further integrates with payment apps, just take care of buying the tickets for us. Instead of having to follow blogs or artists' social feeds, you'd simply get a message that a band you liked was coming to town, and push yes to automatically buy tickets and have it show up on your schedule.

This is also the development that gets everyone using all of these services. Ever deal with a relative who resembles a goose honking and flapping about because the phone is just too confusing? This makes the promise of the internet and smartphones really and truly available to everyone. If you can turn on a TV or the radio, then you can be served custom content on your device.

The big change for the content industry is this – what happens when there is no more popular content? If we make it so easy to consume via web-connected devices that everyone comes on board, then why would we need channels at all? Or critics? Or any of the other current organizing principles for content? Why would you want to create any sort of hit, when you know it would be recommended to a handful of people?

Obviously, we wouldn't give up agency about our cultural choices altogether – if a friend whose taste I trust recommends something, I'm likely to search it out, even if it might not be in my wheelhouse. I discovered the Last Alaskans, a show about people living in the middle of nowhere in Alaska, because a TV critic I like praised it, even though on its face it doesn't sound like something I'd enjoy. But if we are generally enjoying a steady stream of good content, we're probably less likely to seek other things out.

We've certainly already seen a big decline in mass culture – it is very unlikely a pop star will ever be as big as Michael Jackson was in his prime, or a TV event as widely watched and commented on as Roots was. But the full and deep integration of everything we consider the function of an app today could break that down much more quickly.

## What if Every App Was a Music App?

Last week I wrote about where a world where the only music app is a big "play music" button on your phone, and all of your personal data is seamlessly analyzed in order to serve you the perfect music for that exact moment. This week, I want to spin out something a little different – what if, instead of every app integrating with music, music was integrated with every app.

This comes on the heels of Flipagram's eye-popping $70 million raise, and the announcement that the company has struck deals with all three majors labels, two big indie distributors, and several music publishers. Flipagram, for those of you who don't know, allows users to put a collection of photos together to flip by very, very quickly. It makes the laser lights at an EDM show look slow and sedate. I'm shocked the app doesn't come with a warning that it might trigger a seizure.

But health warnings be damned, the app has hockey stick growth, and many of the users were adding music to their flipagrams, in essence creating little music videos. Plenty of artists are jumping on board to create their own flipagrams, including Zedd, Taylor Swift (of course), and Pitbull (double of course). It's clever as hell, and could be another nice revenue stream for artists who use it.

So, could this be the start of something bigger? Rather than creating standalone music services, what if the future is music being embedded in every service? Rumors are circulating that Facebook is starting some sort of streaming product; when they issued a denial it sounded like something Apple would have said to throw people off course ("the way we see it, it's not a "streaming service," it's a "social music listening platform""). Twitter has had plenty of stutter steps with music (We Are Hunted, RIP) and some talent churn, but that's not to say they couldn't do something interesting if they tried. Instagram could just buy Flipagram and allow users to embed songs with every photo. Soundtracking might have been killed off recently, but maybe they were just too early. Vine just hired someone from Billboard and looks like it is beefing up its music team. Etc, etc.

Not every app needs music, of course. My Chase bank app shouldn't be serving me songs, unless they are very soothing and play around tax time. There's a risk of apps falling prey to gimmicks with music – as fun as it sounds to have a mapping app that played location specific tracks, in reality it would likely be annoying. But there are enough social apps consuming enough of everyone's time that it could account for a serious chunk of music consumption.

In that case, what happens to the streaming services? You'll still need them for workout playlists and road trips (please, please do not use Flipagram while driving), but the amount of user hours could go way down if people start consuming music elsewhere, while doing other things. Why listen to a song when you can listen to a song and look at pictures, or social posts. What if music is a feature after all, and not a product?

I've written about this before, but it's worth pointing out that as Flipagrams become the way more people consume songs, the concept of a song might need to change. Many Flipagrams thus far have been clips of tracks, but what if artists started making music specifically geared to backing Flipagram slideshows, with no goals beyond that? Rather than depending on radio programmers or streaming playlist curators to break a track, an artist made something that was so perfect for Flipagram that it was their breakthrough? Quick, someone write a fifteen-second end-of-summer anthem!

If we embed music into every corner of our lives, then what's the value in having a discrete place to consume it? Streaming services, thus far, have done a very poor job defending themselves when trying to address this question. Spotify killed its app platform and has played down many of its social playlisting features; there is no way to interact with or remix Spotify beyond creating playlists. Apple Music's Connect feature allows user commenting on artist-provided content, but nothing beyond that, at least not yet.

What if the true use for music is not to be consumed but to act as a platform for further creativity? Sure, organizing a bunch of selfies to flash by over a track isn't exactly painting the Sistine Chapel, but it's something beyond passively consuming a song, and provides an intensely personal connection for the user. It also opens up to pool of potential connected users beyond those who want to create videos or dances, two ways people have personalized tracks in the past.

The other big X factor in all this is how all this personal use can benefit artists. Adding up fractions of pennies from a track backing a social post probably isn't the strongest business model. In addition to striking deals with labels and publishers, apps like Flipagram should start doing deals with ticketing and merch providers to allow people to seamlessly connect with artists out of the app. They could even strike deals with platforms like Huzza, which allow users to "tip" artists they like, a boon for smaller artists or those not on tour.

Flipagram's moves probably won't spell the end for streaming services any time soon, but they should keep an eye on the deal going forward. One way consumption of content is starting to seem antiquated, and if streaming services want to keep up and attract more young listeners, they should start looking at the relationship as a two-way street.

# Actually, It's About Ethics in Playlist Curation

At this point, pretty much everyone recognizes that playlists are one of the biggest ways people consume music on streaming services. Apple's "For You" section offers a solid stream of compilations, from the sublime ("Indie Hits of [year]" is the best for trips back in time) to the somewhat ridiculous (I like Arcade Fire, but do I really need an "essentials" playlist from a band with four albums?). Spotify just launched a new personalized playlists section that people seem to be wild for, and also offers plenty of user and staff curated mixes based on genres and moods. Songza just celebrated a year of Google ownership and appears to be going strong, and user-curated playlist site 8tracks continues to grow and add talent.

But for all the noise around playlists, no one really seems to know how they are actually made, or what rules govern them. Are they editorial or promotional, and do the editorial departments inside big streaming companies operate by the same rules as more traditional journalism outlets? Do the payola rules that govern terrestrial radio apply online? And while songs themselves are copyrighted works, does the order they appear in on a playlist fall under the same rules?

Any established law on this is vague. The most famous case happened in 2013, when Ministry of Sound sued Spotify claiming that it had refused to delete playlists based on Ministry compilations that had been created and shared by users. The case was settled out of court last year, with Spotify agreeing to remove the playlists from its search and blocking new users from following them, but not taking down the playlists altogether. The out of court settlement also meant that there would be no ruling to create any precedent.

Ministry of Sound could have compellingly argued that people would listen to playlists on Spotify rather than purchasing their compilations, and they wouldn't see any of the upside because they owned the rights to very few of the tracks on their compilations. But could Spotify argue that Apple Music, or any other streaming service, was costing them users by posting identical playlists?

In some cases, playlists on different services appear similar or ever identical because there are only so many tracks available. The Billboard Hot 100 is the Hot 100, no matter who posts it, and anything defined by charts or specific eras and genres is bound to have some crossover. Ditto for mood playlists – there are only so many indie rock songs that are great for working out, especially when you take into account the fact that people want familiar tracks. As more services shift towards human curation, you might expect to see more variety – but then again, there's a certain type of person who loves music enough to score a job as a human curator, and those folks might have pretty similar tastes.

Bad form aside, there's nothing really stopping a service from simply copying playlists and posting them as their own. I have no doubt someone will see this as a shortcut and try to it at some point soon, and I also have no doubt that at some point this will end up in court. But then comes the slippery slope argument – if any playlist can be copyrighted, can every playlist be copyrighted? If I want to take some of the amazing mix CDs I made in high school and turn those into user-generated playlists on a service that allows it, can I then claim that track order as original – and demand payment when someone else listens to it? Services might respond by killing any user generated playlists, which would be a big loss for user engagement.

The other question still to be answered about many playlists is what sort of editorial freedom curators have to add tracks and accept payment for doing so. It generally unclear whether playlists operate like terrestrial radio (as a promotion, with no money allowed to change hands) or the record store endcaps of yore (which were up for sale). And even if official playlists were governed by certain rules, what keeps influencer playlists from being up for sale to the highest bidder? The services could release a code of conduct for users but would have a hard time really policing anything.

On the flipside, if you're going to spend hours putting together amazing playlists and virtually crate digging, don't you deserve to get paid something? Bigger services can afford to hire or at least pay curators, but other sites rely on user-generated playlists, and those cost users time, at least. Again, the user might not have written or recorded any of the tracks on the playlist, but they surfaced them, at least in the case of more obscure lists, and ordered the tracks just so. A great playlist maker is just like a great DJ, in a way, and radio DJs are often paid something.

As curation become more important in a world of unlimited content, it's worth examining what they're owed, and what ethical rules they need to follow. Some blogs are now required to disclose whether they receive any promotional content charge fees to review products, a disclaimer that might be useful if applied to some playlists. Curators are doing important work, and shouldn't be expected to do it for free, but more transparency about how recommendations are made is sorely needed.

## Why Is Live Music Stuck in the Last Century?

Imagine this: it's the summer of 1995, you're 15 years old, and you're about to go see Veruca Salt open for PJ Harvey and Live. You pick up the ticket that you had to adjust your schedule to buy and head off into the crowd, where no one, from the venue owners to the band, has any idea who you are. You watch the show, mildly annoyed at the dude with the disposable camera who won't stop taking pictures, but otherwise have a generally pleasant time. When you leave, you don't communicate any feedback about your experience and the bands never contact you. But hey, they played "Seether" and it sounded awesome!

Fast forward nineteen years. You're, uh, older, and heading out to see Veruca Salt headline the Music Hall of Williamsburg. You paid too much for your ticket on Stubhub because you have a job and adult responsibilities and couldn't reschedule life to navigate the Ticketmaster website. The mildly annoying guy now has a smartphone, but other than that, nothing has changed. The venue and the band have no idea who you are. You never have an opportunity to give any feedback. "Seether" is still a killer song.

While the recorded music business has started to embrace big data, the live space lags far behind. Venues think that because you can't download the experience of being at a live show they'll be insulated from the challenges recorded music has faced, and on a certain level they're right. Live streamed shows are all well and good, but there's no way to really replicate being in the crowd when someone plays your favorite song. The problem is that much of the experience surrounding that one great moment has become so lousy that it might just not be worth it any more.

So what would a truly modern and connected concert experience look like? Let's start with the process of finding out about the show and getting tickets. Though there are plenty of great startups out there trying to solve the first problem, no one has fully mastered the art of making recommendations seamless and keeping you on top of who is coming to town. In smaller markets it's still pretty easy to scan the local alt-weekly and find all the info you need, but in major markets like New York and London, the sheer number of shows happening on a given night can overwhelm the most dedicated fan. Some streaming services, like Spotify, include live music listings; others, like Apple Music, don't. Depending on how you listen, the whole process can feel disconnected.

Even if you have decent recommendations, there's still the cumbersome process of buying tickets, including the need to be online at a certain time to actually attempt to make the purchase. What if there was a way to put down a percentage of the cost of the ticket and then have a machine complete your purchase for you if you weren't able to be online at a given time? I'd love to see AmEx presales go the next step and offer promotions for users to be able to enter a lottery so that they don't need to be in front of the laptop when tickets go on sale.

Then there's the secondary market, which is a great example of free market capitalism in its purest form and a terrible user experience for those of us who don't like paying hundreds of dollars to see a band. It's also terrible from a data perspective, because it creates yet another pool of information on fans that just seems to sit around, unused. The obvious answer would be for ticketing companies to launch their own reselling operations, if just to keep users in one place.

Let's say you finally get everything sorted and get to the show – where the venue will likely look the same as it does almost every night. If venues worked with ticket sellers to gather data on the folks coming to the concert, they might be able to create an audience profile and adjust the atmosphere based on that. Even the zip codes associated with the credit cards could give some indication of what the crowd wants to drink or whether they'll be able to stay out late or need to be home to relieve the sitter. Get social data in the mix, and then we're cooking.

Maybe there's an influencer coming the show – send them a push notification with the offer of a free drink if they share their experience with their followers. If you see that the audience is mostly female, beef up outside security and offer to walk people to their cars. I realize this next suggestion dips into some nastier territory, but if someone's social profile indicates that they're a troublemaker or a predator, it's worth passing along to security to keep an eye on things.

This data can also be used to keep communication flowing during the show. People spend an awful lot of time staring at their phones during concerts, so push notifications are a great way to spread information and keep the audience engaged. You can send quick polls to make sure everything is copacetic and keep folks up to date on set times, wait times, and all the other necessary info.

Any band worth their salt would love to have this data. We've all seen the sad little sign up sheet on the merch table asking for email address – you know, it's the same one bands have had since the late nineties. There's no reason the band can't message the audience before, during, and after the show to solidify their connection and offer rewards.

The live music business can keep on cruising for a while longer, but eventually, it'll run out of gas. Super fans will still show up, but the casual fan will be drawn to experiences that feel more inclusive and rewarding. It's not too late for the industry to start experimenting with data and connecting with their customers, but they need to act fast.

## Why Aren't More Artists Using Twitch?

A few years ago, I was hanging out with the head of an indie label and complaining that one of his artists blew off an interview we had scheduled. The artist told me that he was "too busy" and would need to speak another time. When he heard this, the label head laughed hysterically; the artist in question spent most of the time he wasn't playing live or recording parked on his tour bus couch, smoking pot and playing video games. "Too busy" probably meant that he was about to beat a level and didn't want to take a break.

I bring this up not to bust this artist's balls, but to point out a potential revenue stream that many artists are missing out on – Twitch. The site, which launched in 2011 as a spin-off of Justin.tv and acquired by Amazon a year ago for almost a billion dollars, allows users to play games live while others watch, and the viewers and gamers to interact. Top Twitch users can bring in significant money, and even small time gamers can take donations and make a little extra beer money. Beyond the money, one user told me, it's a way to meet people and make friends who share similar interests.

So far, very few artists have done anything with Twitch. A few, like Deadmau5 and Imagine Dragons, are powers users, and the site has also partnered with Boiler Room and Ultra to livestream events and hosts a library of pre-cleared tracks for gamers to use. But given the number of artists who at least know how to navigate an Xbox, it's a small drop in the bucket.

Twitch can certainly be intimidating to even talented gamers – the site hosts some of the best players in the world, and watching them burn through challenging games can be intimidating. But once you get below the top tier, there are plenty of hobbyist gamers who just like to hang out, and if they happen to lose a level, it's not the end of the world. On a few of the channels I observed, the game was almost secondary, a jumping off point for chatter about other topics. And that's exactly why artists should be embracing Twitch – because it's another platform for them to communicate with fans and to monetize that communication.

Most artist/fan communication confers no tangible financial results, although it is often tied to concert attendance and merch sales. But Twitch, like YouTube, allows partners to share in ad revenues from streams, and if you're going to spend time on the tour bus playing Grand Theft Auto, you might as well make a few extra bucks doing it. Not to mention the fact that you humanize yourself to fans as you either burn through a game or flail around. Even if all you do is drive around in GTA and listen to the fake NPR station, your fans will probably enjoy being part of your day.

Twitch's live streaming concert deals also offer monetization options for artists, and that's only the beginning. Imagine how many fans would chip in a little money to watch a band in the studio working on a new album. They could pay a minimum to see the sessions and pay extra for privileges like voting on which version of a guitar track sounds better, or what the first single should be. As the legions of reality TV shows prove, people actually like watching other, more famous people do nothing but sit around and shoot the breeze. Even the least glamorous parts of being in a band (hanging out in the studio, spending hours on a tour bus) seem exciting and sexy to someone chained to a desk all day.

What Twitch can deliver, more than any other platform, is the ability to feel like you're just hanging out with someone. In-person meet and greets are always limited by capacity and often feel rushed and forced – get in, say hi, and keep moving down the line. Even though you're the only person in front of the artist at a given moment, the chance for any real connection is very low. With a platform like Twitch, even if you're one of thousands of of fans watching the band play Call of Duty, or work in the studio, or just goof off and eat dinner, you feel like you're getting to know them on a deep level.

Young fans have shown time and time again that they want stars to be imperfect and relatable. The most popular YouTubers often joke about how messy and goofy and quirky they are, to the point where it almost seems like shtick for some of them. But they inspire fierce loyalty for those same reasons, because fans see them as friends and not media creations passed down from on high to be consumed. In an ever crowded music space, where choices are virtually endless, showing fans that you're just like them is a valuable move.

I'm not suggesting that artists need to give up all privacy and live like reality stars, unless that's what they want. But it does make sense to take what is essentially wasted time and try to use it to the best of their advantage, and maybe even make a little money off it. The only thing I would caution against is spending time as a user on Twitch – not because it isn't interesting, but because your day will disappear before you know it.

**The Discovery Dead End**

I'll admit to being in a little bit of a new-music rut lately – I haven't had a ton of time to stay on top of the usual blogs and playlists, and traveling frequently means I miss lots of shows and festivals. A few weeks ago, I decided to remedy that situation and find some great new artists to listen to and support, and jumped back on the two streaming services I use (Spotify and Apple Music) itching to become a fan again.

Oh, if only it were that easy. On my first attempt, I subscribed to Apple Music's "The A-List: Indie" playlist and was served a song by a new (to me, at least) band called Teen Daze. I loved it and wanted to engage more, and that's when I ran straight into a brick wall. When I opened the song up to full screen, the only options I got were "Add to My Music," "Show in iTunes Store," "Share Playlist," "Share Song," and "Add to Playlist." No way to get more songs from the band. No way to get more information about the band, or follow them on socials, or even follow them on Apple's own Connect platform. When I clicked over to Connect to see if they were at least suggested, I was confronted with the same recommended list I got when I signed up – Maroon 5, One Direction, and Pitbull, artists I have never listened to. Finally I just plugged the band's name into Google and manually followed them on socials, because I had no other option.

Spotify wasn't any better. I fired up my personalized playlist and got a track from the Tallest Man on Earth, which I quite liked. At least Spotify gave me an easy link to other tracks and a bio – but no links to socials, concert tickets, or merch. I could also easily follow him in Spotify – but that would only serve when I was in Spotify, and not on any other social platforms. And in this case I was listening on my laptop and had time to poke around – if I'd been listening on mobile and jogging or driving, and unable to click around, the song would have just passed me by.

"Discovery" has certainly been the buzzword for the last few years, but the problem is that we still haven't figured out the next steps after someone hears a song. I listen to music all day long but not much of it sticks with me, just because I get no direction from streaming platforms. I have to manually search for artists I like when I'm listening at home, and I have to actually remember to go back through a playlist and search for an artist if I hear something I like when I'm out. And I'm someone who cares about music more than most people.

There are a couple of possible remedies for this. One, streaming services could offer more links out to follow artists on other platforms. Spotify and Apple Music both have their own internal platforms, so I certainly understand why they want to keep people in the services – the problem is that both these internal platforms kinda stink. The artists I follow on Apple Connect put up maybe a video a month, something that I could get on pretty much any other platform, so I have zero reason to engage there. And following artists on Spotify only means I get notified in Spotify when they post something – not great if I'm not always using Spotify. I know you all want your own shiny social networks to keep people engaged, but either make them a whole lot better or kill them altogether.

Artists have their own role to play in this as well, and it usually means offering fans many paths to connection. A buddy of mine recently found a song he loved on Spotify and went off to search for the artist, only to find Facebook and Twitter accounts that hadn't been updated in months and a website that didn't even exist. He didn't want to buy an mp3 or t-shirt and the artist wasn't touring, so had no way to support someone whose music he liked in a meaningful way. Even if you live in a major market, artists only tour through a handful of times every year, and at a certain age wearing your favorite band's shirt ceases to be cool. There need to be options in between.

I wrote about Twitch last week and still think any artist with a PlayStation and some free time should be using it, if only to monetize otherwise wasted hours. But there are also some great virtual tipping services (Huzza, Streamium) that also deserve a look, and any number of ways to sell small things that aren't traditional merch, or launch some sort of affiliate relationships that'll allow fans to shop and support you.

In the end, just being "discovered" on a playlist doesn't mean much to an artist. If services truly want to help artists monetize and build careers, the least they can do is direct listeners to other opportunities to follow, engage with, and support the artist. But artists also have a role to play, by making sure that their content is worth engaging with. If both sides play their parts, it'll be better for them – and for the fans.

## The Creative Nonpocalypse

Last weekend, the New York Times ran a piece called "The Creative Apocalypse That Wasn't", which used employment data to make a case that the predicted decline of arts careers in the digital age hadn't come to pass. Predictably, the responses from the music industry rolled in, including a thoughtful piece from my former editor Rob Levine in Billboard. Both pieces are worth reading, but they also both miss a number of key points.

First, both pieces operate off of a narrow definition of "creative work." The New York Times piece focuses on a giant data set that includes professional athletes, and then a smaller data set of self-employed musicians; Levine's refutation responds to these stats. What's being left out here is the massive number of creative workers who have jumped from self-employment into other creative professions – careers that didn't exist before the rise of the internet.

Take Bruce Henderson, for example. In 1999, he was a self-employed musician and writer who was booked on Letterman – surely something that would boost his career into the stratosphere. He played the Late Show and sold a grand total of 80 copies of his latest album. Around the same time, he started working at a fledgling website called agency.com. He was doing creative work, some of it musical, just in a different place. Henderson stayed in the advertising world, eventually become the chief creative officer for North America of Geometry Global. When I spoke to him last month, he was calling from his beach house, so you can guess how things worked out for him.

One thing that's been largely left out of all these discussions is that there are more avenues to make a living doing creative work than ever before. Almost every day I run by the new Vice offices, which take up almost an entire block in Brooklyn. They employ plenty of creative people to make music and films – and they barely existed fifteen years ago. Ditto for any number of agencies and web design shops that hire artsy types to bring their creative minds to work.

Even for artists who don't want to get a day job, there are more options now than before. Take Matt and Kim, an indie pop duo who haven't sold many records but have worked with tons of brands and made the rounds on the festival circuit. Before 1999, artists shunned big brands for the most part – but now, bands are expected and even encouraged to partner with brands in order to make money. The rise of other creative industries, including the golden age of TV and the exploding video gaming market, also present opportunities for musicians to license and monetize their creative work. And while plenty of startups taketh away, a few also giveth – for example, Flipagram. Artists can now monetize when people use their music to score a photo slideshow or video – something that wouldn't have been possible even a few years ago.

The other main failure of the Times piece and the responses is that the data they look at is limited geographically. As someone who has done a fair bit of data journalism, I completely understand the desire not to wade through international data sets, and since the Times is an American publication with a largely American audience, keeping the focus narrow was a fair choice. However, it means a huge part of the story was left out.

Consider, for a moment, the case of Spoek Mathambo, a South African producer and rapper. Born and raised in Soweto, he rose to prominence when his spooky remix of the Joy Division song "She's Lost Control" and the accompanying video blew up on YouTube; he signed to Sub Pop Records and has worked on a documentary series with Vice.

Would any of this have been possible before the web? Sure, there were international artists, but they had to go through gatekeepers to find broader distribution and a global audience. In Mathambo's case, he was able to build his career on his YouTube popularity – no international distribution deal needed. All he needed was a laptop, a camera, and some recording software.

For artists in certain countries, the web has made all the difference in the world. Ayham Homsi is a musician and producer in Saudi Arabia – a country where playing music in public is largely illegal. Before the web, he could have maybe recorded albums and given copies to friends; now, he posts his tracks on Soundcloud and YouTube for the whole world to hear.

It's always worth looking at who remains silent in many of these debates; while some Western artists have vocally opposed streaming, you don't hear artists from developing markets doing the same. Maybe the heart of the debate about the new creative economy is this – are creators who were in power for so long willing to secede some of that power if it means other voices can be heard?

Is it true that some artists have a harder time making a living than they did fifteen years ago? Absolutely. Is it also true that other artists have been able to make a living where they never could have before? Yes. We now operate in an economy where flexibility is key, and if you expect to keep making a living the same way your entire career, you're going to have a hard time. This doesn't mean that we should ignore copyright and condone piracy, nor does it mean that artists and their supporters shouldn't advocate for fair compensation. But to suggest that creative workers are doomed in the current market vastly overstates the case.

## Too Much Is Never Enough

Recently, many critics have taken to complaining about the fact that there is just too much content floating around out there. Some of the complaints, like those lodged on a recent Grantland podcast, are smart and measured; others, like those in a series of New York Times op-eds bemoaning that a cool record collection doesn't get you laid anymore, less so. Regardless, they all seem to boil down to the same argument – there are far fewer gatekeepers than there once were, and because of that, a lot of terrible content gets made and shared where it wouldn't have otherwise.

I watched the VMAs last weekend for reasons that are still unclear to me, and I'll admit to spending most of the time frantically Googling the names of people on the screen. I learned far more about YouTube and Vine stars than I ever wanted to, as well hearing a bunch of pop songs that I somehow managed to miss this summer. Then I spent some time thinking about the 1995 VMAs, and how many of the celebrities there were mainstream famous actors and musicians that even my parents would recognize. I'm pretty sure if I mentioned Vine to my parents, they would probably think it had something to do with gardening.

So, fine, I'm officially old and all the stuff the kids like baffles me. But lost in all the discussions about this is the following: we have more ways to share content now than ever before, and that means more people have opportunities to share content than ever before. I'll keep beating this drum until my arms fall off: this is, on balance, a good thing. It might be bad for a select number of people, but it's great for many, many more.

Take TV, for example. One of the best shows of the summer is UnReal, which is a pretty explicitly feminist show about how screwed up reality TV can be. It's smart and mean and airs on Lifetime, of all places; you know, the channel that usually shows "Mother, May I Sleep With Danger?" But because the bar for TV is being raised all the time, Lifetime jumped in and ran the show. Ditto Mr Robot, on USA, a channel not known for dark programming. Or the brilliant and woefully under-rated Halt and Catch Fire – even five years ago, would a network have aired a show about two women running a gaming company?

There's more good TV now than ever, and I can understand why some people are burned out. My Netflix queue is always a mile long, and I'm constantly getting recommendations on what to watch next. But again, this is a much better position to be in than having nothing to watch at all. It also means that more stories get told than ever before, and this includes stories about women, people of color, LGBTQ people, and people from all around the world.

The DIY aspect of all of this means that people don't have to jump through hoops to build their fame. A reader of my last piece was critical of the fact that I said all you need is a laptop and an idea to make it big, and I'll amend that slightly – you also need to know how to market yourself and have a personality. But then all you need is a laptop and smartphone and social media. Are crazy parkour Vines my thing, personally? No. Are they someone's thing? Sure, and I'm glad they exist for that audience.

In music, we've been hearing this complaint since the dawn of Napster and bedroom recording applications. The complaints go something like this: now anyone can make music, and we don't have rock critics and record store clerks to tell us what's good, so the world is ending. Now conjure up images of record label presidents, rock critics, and record store clerks, and think about why many of those people tend to look the same. Yeah, there's plenty of terrible music out there now – but there's also a lot of good music that would have never been heard. You have to sift, but so what; the odds of hearing a fresh voice are a lot higher now, too.

There's also an undertone of "I'm not getting the attention I deserve" in many of these complaints. No one deserves attention, just like no one deserves fans. If someone from another culture can do something better than you can, well, them's the breaks in the new economy. No one has the absolute right to live in the world that suits them the best, especially at the expense of others.

At the end of the Grantland podcast referenced above, the hosts both talk about analysis paralysis when it comes to their viewing and listening options – and when you have unlimited choices, it does become easy to revert to the same old things you know you'll love. A few thoughts on this: one, there's nothing wrong with cultural comfort food. Not being the mood to explore or discover is fine, as long as you don't find yourself in a total rut. And even if you do, who cares? You're probably missing some neat things, but it's not like there's a pop quiz at the end of each album or TV season that you have to ace in order to keep existing.

Two, you're never going to get to the end of Netflix or Spotify. And again, that's fine. There's no next level you advance to after watching every prestige drama or listening to every album that Pitchfork likes. Not knowing about Vine stars or YouTube sensations is acceptable. What's not acceptable is romanticizing a world where these people and options don't exist. There's no "either/or" in the world of entertainment – because a terrible song exists, it doesn't cancel out a great song. There is only "and" – and infinite options with something for everyone.

## How Can Social Networks Master Music?

Recently, Vine announced a suite of features that allow users and artists to add music to their videos and discover new tracks. A few months earlier, Flipagram raised a huge round to go after music in a big way, striking deals with artists and positioning themselves as the new social hub for artists to connect with fans. But other popular social networks and social apps haven't quite figured how to crack music; sure, they've all got artists on board, but none of them are doing anything really ground-breaking. Arguably, the most important social network for music remains the late, lamented MySpace, which still technically exists, but come on.

It doesn't have to be this way. There are all sorts of clever and creative things social apps could do in the music space. The following are just ideas, and I'll state upfront that I haven't spoken to any of the folks at these companies, so if these are actual things that will launch soon, great minds and lucky guesses, etc.

We might as well start off with the grandaddy of them all, **Facebook**. At some point Facebook probably looked at the mess MySpace became and decided to avoid betting too big on music, for obvious reasons. That's all well and good, but Facebook is now enough of a global, established brand that it could take some risks in music and not really suffer if they don't pan out. Rumors have flown about a streaming service in the site, which at first seems like a terrible idea, but consider how mainstream Facebook's audience is. Outside of certain territories like the Nordics, the audience for music streaming services is still pretty young, whereas Facebook's audience varies wildly in age (anyone whose Nana likes every picture they post can attest to this). Maybe Facebook doesn't need its own service, but what if it partnered with another service and baked something in, in order to reach an older audience.

The other thing Facebook could do is make the homepage more verticalized, with music as a vertical. I realize there is a way to do this now, but it takes extra steps and isn't exactly intuitive – if you could scan updates from artists you follow (and friends, and celebs, etc) in different tabs, maybe artist posts wouldn't disappear into the mass. A more lean-back experience when it comes to finding out about tour dates and appearances would also be helpful; rather than having to search for dates, I could just get an invite whenever a band I like is coming to town.

**Twitter** and **Instagram** both have the same problem – sure, plenty of artists use the service, and some use it better than others, but none of them go beyond simply using it to create a unique experience for fans. I'm not saying some artists don't create very cool content, but they create the same type of cool content that an actor or athlete or interesting person creates. Nothing in the ecosystem sets musicians or music apart.

In Twitter's case, they seem to be leaning on Vine for this, which is fine, but doesn't go far enough. They could certainly experiment with a more lean-back experience, especially for artists who don't tweet that often. I follow some great artists on Twitter who rarely post anything, and often wind up missing on song releases or shows because they fail to say anything. If Twitter could look at the artists I follow and send me notifications in my stream about their upcoming releases or events in my area, that would be less work for artists and great for fans.
Twitter has also gone big on major events, which is great, but what about smaller events? I was at Irving Plaza in New York last night for the L7 show – not a giant event by any stretch of the imagination, but one that I wanted to socialize and view other people's social content. Aside from the search feature, which is often inaccurate with certain popular terms, and hashtags, which plenty of people don't use, there's not a great way to look at all the content around an event. Maybe if there was some way to Storify an event so it could be easily monitored in real time, and facilitate connections at the show. Artists could even get in on it and use it to take requests and poll fans.

**Instagram** has plenty of artists as well, but again, nothing separates them from athletes or models or just a person taking a snap of their brunch. One of the biggest problems, again, lies in the feed, and the fact that it's simply chronological and all mixed together. It's hard for me to create verticals to view content and make sure it doesn't pass me by, and it's hard for me to share content within the app – especially important for artists who want to engage with fans by sharing particularly good fan-created content.

Aside from that, the biggest flaw in Instagram is that you can't add music to images or video (at least legitimately; you can certain film something with music in the background). Flipagram's numbers have grown exponentially in the last year and there's clearly a demand to marry music and photo and video content, so it's odd that Instagram hasn't jumped on board. Even if artists were able to embed a song clip in a still image, it would be a huge differentiating factor.

All three major social platforms have done a great job on-boarding artists, but now it's time to take some next steps and make music stand out. People are so deeply invested in music and have such a deep connection to it – and anything that helps make that connection stronger is a win for these companies.

# The Fundamental Why of Music Discovery

*Everyone seems to be betting big on music discovery. What if they're wrong?*

These days, it seems like everyone has an opinion of the best way to discover music. Apple focuses on human curation with intricate playlists and Beats1 Radio. Google thinks that's all elitist nonsense and that machine learning will solve the riddle. Pandora has a proprietary algorithm. A startup that claims to be "Product Hunt for Music" just got accepted into Troy Carter's accelerator. Hype Machine fights the good fight and scans the blogs. There are websites, there's Soundcloud, there's a ton of failed startups to help you find the best new indie music first.

And I suppose that's fine, except no one has figured out what the end goal of all this discovery is, or whether that's what people even want in the first place. There are surveys that float around stating that people stop discovering music after college, or in their thirties, or after they have kids, but the definition of discovery is never clear. Does simply hearing a song mean I've "discovered" it. If so, my nana is "discovering" music every time she goes to the grocery store, even though she's unlikely to ever engage any further with it. Does "discovery" mean I have to take a next step, like seeking out more songs by an artist, or visiting their website, or buying concert tickets? If so, that filter gets awfully narrow very quickly.

"Discovery" has become to music what "engagement" has become to brands – a buzzword that means absolutely nothing. The arms race for shares on socials has gotten so out of control in the brand world that it almost doesn't matter whether or not people are spending money on the brand – as long as the identity is strong, and people are talking, that's what matters. In music, being on a popular playlist, or Beats1, or the top of the Hype Machine charts means...something. No one is quite sure what, though.

The removal of the need to purchase a physical good from the process is arguably the worst thing to happen to music discovery. Now, I love streaming music and would never want to return to the days of driving to a store to pay fifteen dollars for an album that may or may not be good – but at least there was a fairly easy action to signal whether or not you were interested in a band. It was an action that was available to almost everyone (unlike going to a live show, which depends on geography and ability to be free a certain evening) and it meant that you were likely to keep engaging with the band, because if you pay for an album, chances are you're going to listen to it multiple times.

Now, we can just keep dipping into playlists and never repeating any tracks. There is an endless world of music at our fingertips, but that makes it feel totally ephemeral, and not much seems to stick. Unless we go way down the funnel and buy tickets or merch, our engagement means very little to the artist. We're also spoon-fed content rather than having to go out and search for it, so we don't put any effort in – we just hit the button and go, and we're less invested because we know we'll always be served another track in a few minutes.

But we can debate the mechanics of discovery until the end of time and never address the central question – why do people want to discover music in the first place? I realize it sounds very simple, and the answer, "to have something the listen to," very obvious. But is that really the case?

When kids and teens discover music, it's partly because they want something to listen to, and partly because they want a way to define themselves. The cliques at my high school were all the established tropes – the pop kids, the hip-hop heads, the grunge kids (it was the nineties), the punks, the sensitive indie kids (it was Portland). We defined ourselves by the music we liked because there were so few other ways to define ourselves – you could talk about the movies you loved or the games you played, but this was before the real rise of the internet, so options were limited.

Today kids still shape their identities around music, but they also have many other channels to help craft their personal narrative. They can emulate YouTube or Vine stars or shape themselves as artsy and hip because they watch foreign films on Netflix all the time. There's no doubt that many kids still love music and it touches them in meaningful ways, but the level of urgency seems to be less than it once was.

Once you move out the phase when music defines you and on the phase where your career and dating status take care of that, the need for new music becomes even more nebulous. This isn't to say that you can't find comfort and community in music once you hit a certain age – I'm thirty-five and wept like a baby when I listened to the latest Sufjan Stevens album – but the hunger for new tracks does seem to fade.

So is music discovery the future and driving force behind so many music startups for any real reason, or is it just an organizing principle everyone seems to agree on? "Serving you stuff you already know and like" doesn't sound all that great, and certainly sounds like a downer in future focused startup circles. But if "discovery," which so many people have sunk so many resources into mastering, isn't the future...what is?

# The Unrealized Promise of Apple Music Connect

Next week brings a major milestone for Apple Music – three months after launch, free trials will start running out and users will have to decide whether it is worth $9.99 a month to stick with the service. The product has gone from a splashy launch at the end of June to not even warranting a mention at the last Apple event, and one high profile exec has already departed, admittedly for what sounds like an unturndownable dream job at a luxury brand in Paris.

I've been using Apple Music since it launched, almost daily, and I still generally like it. There are certainly bugs that need to be worked out – for instance, playlists I subscribe to don't update unless I unsubscribe and resubscribe, which is annoying – but the overall experience is solid. Their curated playlists are generally on the nose, although the app doesn't match Spotify in terms of new music discovery. The "New" section is still unwieldy and overwhelming. The radio offerings, particularly the hyped Beats1, are high quality, although some of the excitement has worn off. I personally don't love the DJ chatter, but that's just me. In terms of the programming, it remains top notch.

Where Apple Music has fallen short, though, is with Connect. Not many artists on there, and those that are don't post much content. There's no real reason to engage with Connect at all, which is a shame and huge missed opportunity. For all that it does well, Apple has still failed to help artists take the next steps in connecting with fans.

It doesn't have to be this way. None of the existing social networks are perfect for artists – Facebook is too sprawling; Twitter too limited in terms of content and the stream too ephemeral. Instagram is clean and simple but doesn't provide anything unique for musicians. Flipagram is still a relative upstart. Vine only works with a small handful of artists. Connect would be a real opportunity to create something great, but it seems stuck in neutral.

First off, Connect needs to figure out what its value proposition is. Right now it simply...exists. It's as if someone on the team said "we need a social network because...we need one" and built it from there. Is Connect's purpose to provide exclusives (which generally make it to other outlets in under ten minutes and negate the whole point of the thing)? Is it to break news? To sell tickets or merch? To create a community for artists and fans to interact with each other?

The last value proposition is, I believe, the strongest. Now, there are theoretically tons of platforms for artist and fan community engagement in the market already – but none of them are that good. There's too much noise and they all turn out to basically be a one-way street, with many fans shouting at an artist and the artist occasionally replying. They are also divorced from the act of listening to music – if an artist tells you about great new music on another social platform, it's harder to get to it and then follow leads than it could be in Connect.

What Connect could do is narrow the circle. For instance, it could use the data it already has on how much someone listens to an artist, and cross-reference it with other social data, and figure out who an artist's most valuable fans in Apple Music are. From there, it could grant access to those fans, showing them content or letting them chat with the artist at given points. If Connect is also upfront with users about how they could access those special perks, engagement would grow because other users will want to participate. This is a direct path from discovery to engagement, and it'll both differentiate the service and make it stickier. For artists, it provides an incentive for people to listen to their music more – which means more money.

The other place Connect could iterate is connecting fans with one another. No other social network has been able to crack that code – it's why, even with all the apps we visit daily, people say one of the biggest reasons they don't go to events is because they have no one to go with. If Connect could be a platform for fans to share, make plans, and meet each other, it could prove very valuable and, again, sticky. Just putting up a video once a week or hosting an event every so often won't keep anyone coming back – but offering a place where people can form meaningful bonds will.

In a way, Connect could become almost like a political campaigning organization for artists. It sounds odd, but many musicians could learn quite a bit from grassroots political campaigning – namely, superserve your biggest supporters and let other supporters be your voice, because you can't be everywhere. Political campaigns have some of the strongest community bonds and most loyal folks, because people are rewarded for connecting with others and bringing them into the fold. If Connect can marry data with outreach opportunity, it could be something new and game-changing for artists.

Even if Connect doesn't go down this road, it needs to figure out something, and fast. The last thing anyone wants is another Ping, which somehow managed to hang on for two years before folding. Connect has all the money and resources behind it that one could possibly ask for, as well as the Apple name and a streaming service that's pretty darn good. If the folks behind Connect can't take this and build something pretty cool with it, they'll have squandered a huge chance to create something great.

# Conversations

## Alina Simone

In the wake of her New York Times op-ed "The End of Quiet Music," I chatted with musician and writer Alina Simone. I first met Alina in 2005 when we both worked for a performance measurement consulting firm, and we might be the only two people in the music industry with master's degrees in public policy. In her op-ed, Alina bemoans the need for musicians to constantly hustle and be entrepreneurial, citing a unique case – women in post-communist Russia who struggled after their day jobs disappeared. Even though the women were given grants and business training, they missed the days when they had stable, structured gigs. We also talked about the myth of the artist as entrepreneur and how to make music more sustainable.

CH: There was a lot in your essay that resonated with me, but I think the point you started off with about the Russians who you met who preferred working in a factory over owning their own businesses struck me really hard. A lot of people are sort of crying about the whole startup economy that lets anyone launch anything, and anyone can have their own business, and it's so great, but a lot of people don't actually want that. And now I feel like we have something that's called "social second shift," and that's that you have to go out and network all the time, you have to go to events, you have to be connected – and that's in addition to doing your actual job. And that's not everyone's cup of tea. There are people who would just like to do work and that's all they do. How do you answer the people who say "If you can't hustle, you shouldn't play music and then you should just go do something else."

AS: Well, I would invite them to imagine a world where every actor had to fundraise his own movie, and every ballerina had to create her own ballet company, and every author had to form his own publishing company. I mean, maybe there are people sitting behind their laptops somewhere thinking that snarky thought, but I think that way the world has become increasingly entrepreneurial, it's harder and harder to insulate yourself from this new reality, no matter what business you're in. I was very hesitant to publish that essay. I sat on it for a very long time.

And I almost withdrew it. Because I felt like I was almost going to open myself to a flood of criticism just as you described: "Well, if you can't stand the heat, get out of the kitchen." You know? It's a Darwinist world out there, and only the best survive. But instead I found there was an extremely positive response, and I think it was just because everyone has been feeling that pressure. I don't think it was even specifically about the music industry, I think it's just that everyone feels stressed out and sort of pressured to be entrepreneurial, whereas that's not a quality that everyone has or even should have. It's become this weirdly prioritized value that I don't think deserves its enshrined status that it's currently enjoying.

CH: You have a child, and even though you don't discuss this in the piece, I think it's an important part of the story, because it's pretty hard to be out there socializing and hustling when you have to go home and take care of your baby or be a parent. And I really feel like this current mentality of "Oh, just rely on Kickstarter, just be an entrepreneur – go found a startup! Create your own job!" really privileges the young and the urban and the childless, because if you're a parent, you have to think about health insurance, and being available to take care of your child, and maybe you can't afford to live in New York City or San Francisco and have a child. This very flip, "Oh, just go start your own thing, it'll be fun, it'll be an adventure, and if you fail, just go start another thing," a lot of that mindset is the privilege of young, single people in their twenties.

AS: Yeah, exactly. And I mentioned in my book, in my essay collection, that this sort of reality check for me came when I was around 35 and I was thinking about having a child, and I got included on some kind of best-of list, Best Solo Singer best-of list, and I saw that on this list, all of the singers on it, only one had a child. And you can go down this list – and it's like - PJ Harvey, Neko Case, Cat Power. They're really familiar names. And if you dig deeper, and you look into interviews with these women, it's like – a lot of them say they want a child. Or that they wanted one. Maybe it's too late now. But that's not something that they had ruled out or made a conscious decision to avoid. But I think the lifestyle that you're forced to adopt is wholly incompatible with raising a child. I think that it becomes a whole sacrifice, and one that's made primarily by women, because we all know most all of the male indie rockers of a similar age have families. I don't see the same phenomenon happening with 40-year-old male singer-songwriter types.

CH: Yeah. That's exactly it. And you mentioned Cat Power – she went broke, as well. And she had a lot of other issues and problems that led to her being broke but – again, I think you look at someone like her – can she go crowdfund an album? Can she go crowdfund her rent, or her car payment, for that matter? What are musicians even expected to – yeah, you can crowdfund making a record, but you can't crowdfund your life, really.

AS: I think that Cat Power is in a much better position to crowdfund her record or her life than people who didn't have the Matador platform to springboard from, because Cat Power is famous enough that she can generate enough pre sales for a new album to fund at least the making of that album, and probably some other things. But I think the other thing that gets overlooked with Kickstarter is that it is a pre sale. That the costs are significant, and the profit is pretty minimal, in a lot of cases. If artists feel like they need another day of recording, because they budgeted x, and that's how much they fundraised, they think that their album's going to be better because they're spending another $2000 in the studio, they're going to do it. And I think people kind of neglect to see – just because you raised $100,000, you didn't make $100,000 in profit, you can't live on that for a year. You just pre-sold items that you have not yet manufactured, shipped, packaged, et cetera. So – I mean, that's why I ended that piece. These are familiar gripes, I think, about Kickstarter and the realities of the economics of being a musician. But that's one issue of other institutions adopting that, right now, don't include musicians as a group to support, including academia, government, arts funding, philanthropic arts funding organizations – they don't see pop music as art. And I think that there is that category of whatever, booty-shaking, very, very commercial music, that doesn't need the support of those groups and shouldn't get it, probably. But I think it's fair to say, looking out at the musical landscape, that there's a lot that can be considered art, and there's really no legitimate reason why musicians aren't allowed access to those same pretty meager, but still important benefits that artists in other genres aren't entitled to.

CH: It's interesting you mention the big misunderstanding about Kickstarter, or one of the big ones, which is that it's not free money. I feel like that's the old way of viewing that was when an artist would get a major-label advance, and someone would say "Ooh, that artist just got a million-dollar advance, a major-label advance, they must be wealthy now, they're gonna go out and buy a Porsche," and they don't realize that's not free money. You still need to pay that back, or sell enough records against it to pay it back. Just to play devil's advocate for a minute now – the counter-argument to a lot of what you've written is that – you know, musicians are natural self-promoters. Performers are natural self-promoters. 'cause if you didn't want to promote or have confidence in your work, you wouldn't put it out there. What's the difference between sharing a song and then soliciting funding in order to be able to share the song?

AS: Right. I think, first of all, what got cut from my piece, because those op-ed pieces have a pretty strict word count – what got cut from my piece was sort of the specifics of what I had to do to put out that album, and the costs that I cut, such as radio promotion, which, if you go to an agency, will run you easily $1500 minimum and up to $3500 if you want to hit every radio station in the country – that's something that I did, for instance, all by myself. I just got friends to give me the list of every indie college station, and I personally wrote emails to every music director on the list, and personally sent those CDs to them. And, I mean, in part, it was just because I was really watching my budget – I can't afford to pay a promoter $3500, or even $1500, and I'm just going to do this myself and it's just going to cost a couple of hundred dollars. So, I think that when you see this itemized list, I think you'll see how far beyond self-promotion it goes, because the truth is that I was far from a shrinking violet. I was out there booking shows, touring the country, doing all of the work of self-promotion that every artist has to do just to maintain a presence in the musical landscape. I mean, there's definitely a baseline, and I think that that baseline is actually pretty high, that you've gotta really gin up whatever extroversion you can manage, because you do have really got to flog your work there. But when my labels folded, it went so much beyond that. I really felt like I was starting my own business in that way that these women in Russia who were laid off were forced to start their own businesses, and go into debt in order to do it, and microcredit was really nice name for debt. And it always stuck with me, that reminder of spending that summer talking to these women, because everything that I'd been taught when I got out into the field, all of these wonderful NGO concepts and theories, were so far from the reality. The women I spoke to – they just called microcredit loans and debt that they had to pay back. And they were in fact really nervous about this interest accruing and they weren't at all happy that this stable predictable source of income was gone and that they had to hustle all the time. And that really stuck with me. So I feel like it's not just about "Suck it up, you've got to be self-promotional," it's really about "Well, you have to start your own business, and I hope that you're a good business person, and I hope that you're really eloquent and can write your own press releases, and I hope that you're good with spreadsheets, because you're going to have to keep track of every sale, and all of your taxes," and it goes on and on and on to the point where I actually – I don't feel like I'm terrible at any of those things. I can write a press release, and I can use Excel. But when I think about some of my bandmates – I've been in a lot of bands. I've been the singer for a lot of bands in New York. And my bandmates, some of whom were just incredibly musically talented, just as talented as any of the Pitchforkian bands, musicians that we hear about all the time, they were not from the backgrounds that embedded these skills in children, you know? Some of them were from really, really poor backgrounds, and had scraped their way to New York and lived a pretty hand-to-mouth existence and were just super talented. And basically, if it was up to them to do any of this stuff, they would just fold immediately. They wouldn't be able to do it. They needed bandmates to do that stuff for them. When you're solo, you don't have a bandmate. You just have to do it all yourself and you just have to be good at it.

CH: There is a class privilege associated with all of this. Kickstarter's great, but you have to know people with money in order to solicit them, and that knocks out a lot of people. I'm in the startup world, and I hear all these founder stories: "I was broke, and I was this, and I was –" The common one is "I lived on my parents' couch." And I'm like "That's great, but there a lot of people whose parents don't have couches. Their parents don't have homes. There's no one for them to mooch off of while they launch this great idea or this great artistic career, or there's this inherent base level you need even to be quote-unquote "broke".

AS: Yeah.

CH: Nirvana is an example – they were white trash kids. They had no money. And they got funded because they got signed to Sub Pop. And now that avenue's closed up to so many people. And this is a point that gets lost constantly, in so many conversations. People are like "Why don't you just start a startup?" Not everyone has the resources to do that.

AS: It's a very white, upper-middle-class landscape out there. And I think that if you compare – ok, so thirty years ago we had Nirvana, and who do we have now? We have Vampire Weekend. We have The National. We have MGMT. We have groups of white guys who went to Yale, Wesleyan and Columbia. And not to knock their music – I think their music is great. I like catchy songs about bourgeois problems as much as the next guy. But I do think that something is being lost, you know? And I think a whole world of experience is being lost, because, you know, I think when you listen to the songs, and the music that comes out of people who grew up in vastly different circumstances, it's a whole different landscape, too. You don't even realize what you're losing. And I think that's what I was sort of trying to get across in my op-ed, is that I'm not saying that the loss of my music is going to be mourned, but I think a lot of people would really mourn the lack of the next Kurt Cobain, the music that could change their life, because the way things are going now it's becoming really difficult for those people. They're not going to ask their mom who works 2 jobs and can barely pay rent to contribute to a Kickstarter or friends, you know, it's just – when you have experience with real poverty, Kickstarter sort of starts to look like a shame-generating machine or something.

CH: The way that a lot of artists got funded in the past was through idea of patronage – not just from the public but from the government. And we had the culture wars in the '80s around the NEA, and I feel like those have largely subsided. But there's still so few government grants for artists in the US. And if you go to CMJ or South by Southwest, you see the different countries flying their indie artists in. You'd never see that in the US. Is it the government's place to be funding musicians and indie musicians and painters? It's debatable whether it's better or worse than funding starving children, or, more realistically, drones to spy on people, but – is there a role for the government to step in and fund indie musicians, indie artists?

AS: Well, I guess, I'm not arguing about funding health care versus funding art – I would side on the side of health care, but I would also argue for genre equality, which I don't feel is the case now. I feel like there's a real snobbery about pop music that is undeserved and is sort of a holdover from, I don't know, the disco era or the '80s or something, because pop music is not strictly commercial now, there's so much innovation and intelligence and art going on that it no longer seems ethical or logical to deny those artists the same access to resources that other artists in different genres have access to. So that's sort of my argument. I can't understand why a poet or a painter is any more worthy of a grant than an indie musician at this point. I think everything should be judged on its own merits. I don't think songwriting is any less virtuous a subject to be taught at the university level than, you know, poetry, or literary fiction. I think that it's just a genre. It deserves its own space. It deserves to be added to the pantheon. So that was sort of my point – we really need to reevaluate the institutions that support the arts and find room for music, given that there's been such a drastic change in the commercial landscape, and we – all of us – steal and enjoy this music. So it's time to find some mechanisms for musicians to be able to make music.

CH: What about corporate patronage? Twitter's IPO is going to happen soon, and that's going to create a lot of millionaires who are young, hip people who like cool music. Do you think we're ever going to see a point where some Twitter, or Google, or Facebook – you know, pick your startup – millionaire decides "I'm just going to start giving money to cool bands?"

AS: I think that there's plenty of room for innovative nonprofit models, like a non-profit label model. That space is pretty unpopulated. So I think there could be really unique hybrids there, nonprofit labels that still do something with that music that maybe generates some bucks to offset the costs. One of the interesting things that happened after my article came out is I was contacted by Jim Sykes, who is the drummer for Marnie Stern and for a lot of other bands, including his own, and has been an indie musician for a long time, but is also a professor of ethnomusicology at UPenn. And he asked if I'd be interested in helping him put together a conference about these issues specifically. Like, very solution-oriented – how can we interest those new Twitter billionaires in investing in music as an art form in a non-profit label, or a grant-giving institution, or even an awards-giving institution, that would give cash awards to musicians in the same way that the Guggenheim – the trickle-down funding from the NEA at the state level, does. So we're doing it. He's already raising money from UPenn and we've come up with our dream list of speakers and panel participants, and we're really hoping to get the philanthropic community there, both from private foundations and representatives from the NEA. And we would, of course, welcome any new Twitter millionaires who were interested in the subject. But we really want to do more than just sort of reiterate the problems, relying entirely on Kickstarter or rehashing the dismal state of the industry due to piracy. Everyone already knows all of these things. We're interested in moving toward solutions, because I think it is possible to really reshape how institutions view indie music.

## Andy Weissman

Andy Weissman is a partner at Union Square Ventures (USV), one of the most forward thinking and influential VC firms in New York City, whose portfolio companies include Twitter, Soundcloud, and Etsy. Prior to joining USV, he cofounded BetaWorks, which both created and invested in social real-time applications and services; he's also a rabid music fan who regularly posts amazing tracks on his Tumblr page and has great stories about interviewing random indie artists back in the day. When I spoke to him, we talked about how he judges music startups as an investor and as a music fan, and why so few music industry people are making the jump into the startup world.

CH: I wanted to start off by referencing a piece in New York Magazine that I read about another USV portfolio company, which is Twitter. The author refers to "a problem which shouldn't be solved," and in the case of a lot of music startups, I'm seeing something kind of similar, which is that they're solutions to problems which may or may not exist. I worked for an artist chat app called Soundrop; and I doubt there were a lot of people walking around and saying "I wish I had a way to build playlists and chat in real time with my friends" before we were around. But we created that, and people seemed to like it, and they used it. And, likewise, before Twitter, there was no one saying "I wish I had a way to share 140-character updates about my life," but it blew up anyway. It was clearly solving something that people wanted, even if people weren't really naming it. From your perspective, how do you know if a startup is solving a problem people might not know they have versus solving a problem that doesn't exist?

AW: I'm not sure I or anyone will ever know that. That's what kind of makes it fun. I was traveling the past couple of days and I happened to be in Nashville, and I was talking to a group of entrepreneurs, and they asked a similar question. They were asking "As an investor, how do you – how do you evaluate something that may not have existed before and therefore it doesn't represent a problem for people?" And I thought to myself, in a way, people are, human beings are very simple in our base desires and needs. You wake up every day, and you want to feel happy, and you want to feel secure, and you want to feel intellectually stimulated, and you want to laugh, and be moved, and you want to share, and you want people to share with you. And maybe there's five or six or seven base human desires and characteristics. When we talk about services and applications and problems being solved, maybe the problem that's being solved is that they make us feel happier, they enable us to share, they enable people to share with us, they enable us to be stimulated, they enable us to feel better as human beings. And maybe that's the set of problems, and not "Would you like to communicate in 140 characters," you know? Or "Who would like to have a summary of your news?" or "Who would like to share pictures of what people are eating?" And so when you evaluate it like that, it seems silly. A service that allows you to share pictures of your food? That's the dumbest thing I've ever heard. But if you think about it like, well, that's what makes you smile and it reveals the humanity of people, then it feels more like a problem. And I think that's maybe a more interesting lens to look at things around how they affect human beings and what do they do for human beings? This could be in media or this could be in business, it doesn't really matter. It just gets at – what's that base feeling or emotion? Now when we're seven years into the Twitter era, and you say, "Well, would you like a service that will allow anyone in the world to share things with anyone else in the world," you're like "Yeah, actually, that sounds like a good idea." At the time we may not have conceived of it that way or even described it that way. But I think the best services do that for us.

CH: If you're looking at a product or an idea and you're trying to make a decision about whether to fund it or not, is there research involved in terms of – is there an audience for the product? Do you need to know that there's sort of a core group for you to invest, or do you trust that a core group can be built?

AW: I think it's case by case. If you're an investor in the early-stage companies, you're going to take that leap of faith. And that's part of the risk/reward profile in deciding to start a company, to work at an early-stage company or to invest in that company, and I think you can't quantify away that leap of faith. That said, I think you bring to it as an investor these individual ideas and theses and beliefs. And you attempt to test or challenges those ideas and beliefs, and if there's some data about a service that allows you to do that, it could be one user or a million users, it could be a trend, it could be a graph suggesting something, I think you feel more confident in putting your investment dollars against that belief. And sometimes you have more data, and sometimes you have less data. The research that I think is the most meaningful is exactly that, testing those beliefs and those principles you have versus what someone is creating and how people might be using that service. You know, market-size research is imprecise, so it's hard to do, and also I think the best services or applications are ones that either create new markets or expand the size of markets anyway. I'm thinking of Etsy in particular, but there are many others. And so there's probably no market research you could do that could convince yourself those were good – those were large opportunities. And that's where that leap of faith comes in. So I think it's a combination of those things, and each case – each case is different, I think.

CH: There's another common complaint that I hear a lot from people outside the tech sphere, and from blogs like Valleywag and more sort of political folks, and they say, looking at Silicon Valley and New York, they say that a lot of entrepreneurs are focusing on creating these new problems that are fun and exciting and sexy, all about listening to music with your friends or selling cool products, rather than trying to solve these really big existing problems. I know that it's partially probably because it's way more fun to build a collaborative listening app than deal with a lot of government bureaucracy and build an app that helps homeless mentally ill people take their meds on time, or build Obama's healthcare site. But arguably, I think maybe building a really good healthcare site is maybe more important than working on a music app. Do  investors have a role in changing this?

AW: I don't know if I totally agree with some of the premises. I think it's really hard to attempt to extract an overlay on what people choose to spend their time on. I think it'd make you crazy, trying to figure that out, or think that trouble. People are going to do what they're going to do. Here's what I think has happened in the last ten years, or the last seven years. I think for a long time, the internet probably defined – was niche media, right? There was media and then there was new media. Remember, people used to call the internet new media. We don't hear that any more. It was always sort of over on the side. And about five or six years ago, a couple of things happened. Fast broadband smart mobile devices, Facebook, social services – that ended that distinction forever. And this internet that used to be niche became the mass media, right? There was no old media, new media, everything was internet media. And that was a very big cultural change. And part of what happened with that cultural change is people said "I want to work in the internet! I want to be an entrepreneur." The entrepreneur as an archetype really came into being. There were books about entrepreneurs and TV shows about entrepreneurs. I mean, my grandfather was an entrepreneur, but he never would have called himself that, 'cause it wasn't a thing. There wasn't an ecosystem. So everyone's creating things. And the cost to create is essentially zero, right now. We could come up with an app this afternoon. The three of us could build it and launch it. And so you have a lot of energy. And I believe if you could measure the karma value in the world, it's increased by more people who are creating things, regardless of what they're creating. That's a good positive force. Some of those people will choose to spend their time building lots of different things. However, I think that, and I'll wear a USV hat, I think things like Etsy and Kickstarter and Funding Circle and SoundCloud and Twitter are catalysts for social good in ways that may be as meaningful as some of the samples you gave. And there are lots of things like that. And so where that social good comes from may look very differently than when you try to overlay value, a value judgment or a value system, on it. I believe you can be a really good entrepreneur and have a lot of good experience, too. You know, the archetype of the college dropout or the high school dropout is an outlier archetype. I started my first company when I was 40 years old. I don't know if that makes me an entrepreneur, but you don't have to start it when you're 17. I worked for fifteen years before I decided to start something, and I started BetaWorks with my partner John [Borthwick]. So there may be an experiential layer to people that may allow them to build more interesting things rather than finding narrow gaps as you defined. And maybe culture and economy is moving in cyclical shifts, and maybe we're going through a period where it appears where people are not working on important things, and it may appear differently this year or the year after.

CH: I think you make an important point, especially with something like Twitter, or even Vine, or Instagram – those were not created as social change agents, but then they were used in ways that were very meaningful. Look at the revolutions that were tweeted about, or people taking Instagrams or Vine videos of police brutality events that then went viral and are changing the way that a police department conducts their business. I also think the point that you made about the barrier to entry being lower is a really good one, because it's going to allow people who maybe aren't Stanford students or Stanford dropouts to participate. It'll allow someone to say, "I'm an older person, and I have a problem with my health care. I'm not a 17-year-old kid who's super healthy, but I can create an app for older people to manage their medications."

AW: It's almost like the the internet writ large, at a most basic level, just opens up possibilities. And those possibilities don't require the permission of anyone to realize. And that's really good force for social change, what we build upon it, starting with that proposition. And you've worked in a number of these companies, and you've covered the industry from the inside out, and you've worked in companies from the outside in. Think about how fundamentally different the industry is, and music in particular, because we have this network connecting everyone to everyone, and every person to every person, and every artist to every person, and allow for frictionless sharing of media and media objects. One level, music is just music, and on another level, there's social good involved in all music at some level.

CH: Why do you think so few music industry people have made the jump and moved into starting music startups? This is shifting a little bit, but I do feel that the people who are music startup founders are not label people or people with music management experience – do you think this is because the music industry needs these disruptive external forces in order to make these changes, or do you think outsiders still see the music industry as this fun, glamorous, sexy, cool place?

AW: I have this notion that you have DNA, and you work in an industry, and you have DNA, and we all have our own DNA, and that DNA, over time, results in seeing the world a certain way, and it's very difficult, if not impossible, to see it in a new way. And entrepreneurs, definitionally, see things in a new way. Sometimes they're right, sometimes they're wrong. So change comes from the outside, or the edges, not the center, I think. By the way, I think you see this dynamic not just in music but in all businesses, in the way financial services are being completely reimagined on the internet through peer funding platforms and things like that. So I think you just have your certain DNA, and your certain DNA tells you this is how the world is, and it's hard to think of the world in a new fashion. One of the things when we look at investment opportunities in any sector, at a certain level there's almost a facile, binary way of taking a first pass and looking at something, which is some businesses take something that already occurs and make them a little better, and some businesses completely imagine the way they work. And one is not better than the other, they're just two different buckets of things. And oftentimes, if you have too much intimate knowledge of an industry, you'll just sit there and say "I can make this a little better." If you have no knowledge or little intimate knowledge, you will conceive up a completely new way of doing things. And I think that probably occurs across a lot of different businesses. By the way, this happens to us as investors, too. We miss investment opportunities, we pass on investing in companies that turn out to be incredibly large, profitable, meaningful companies, because we couldn't see the world that they imagined, because we thought "Nobody's going to pay $100 to sleep on someone's couch, that doesn't make sense. You're going to go stay in a hotel where you get fresh towels!" That's a real example.

So, you know, so it can happen to all of us. One of the core things in business is that you balance your pattern recognition, which is your way of saying "I seen the way the world works, I know how this movie ends, I see the patterns," and you balance that with your gut, which relies on intuitive sense and there's nothing quantitative about that. Those are opposing forces, but I think that in that mix, that's where meaningful things happen. And so, by the way, this happens to be why my favorite lyric of all time from Lou Reed is "Between thought and expression lies a lifetime," because I think it kind of covers that, right? How do you get to that point where you're balancing what you know with what you feel? Those are not the same things. But I think that you find inspiration in there.

CH: But I do wonder why most music startups don't at least seek advice or learn about the music industry before launching. I'm thinking specifically of [shuttered communal listening site] turntable.fm, which when I first saw it I was like "This is an amazing product, it's super fun, they don't have licenses? They're going to get screwed." And they got screwed. A lot of these startups or great, but shouldn't they at least, or shouldn't the people investing in them at least be like "Hey, you guys, you might want to get a license before you do this?"

AW: This is a really good question, because if you think about the balance between facts and gut – you can get that wrong. And maybe one of the ways you get it wrong is that you don't do enough pattern recognition, you don't do enough research in that industry, you fall on the wrong side. You make the wrong decision. SoundCloud doesn't have any deep, meaningful, formal relationships with the industry, and that works, because they built a product that was consistent with rights holders as well, because if you own the rights you can post it. I think there are cases where you do enough work, and there are cases where you can do too much. I think that one of the powers – and your question was, how come a lot of entrepreneurs don't spend enough time understanding the industry, or talking to people in the industry – I think that one of the things about the internet, one of the things we talk about internally, my partner Brad uses the phrase "permissionless innovation," which is that the internet allows for permissionless innovation. You can build a service, you don't need to ask anyone's permission. You set up an account, you get a domain name, it's empowering of people. When you get into that, as an entrepreneur, asking someone's permission can feel like failure, and sometimes it can be failure.

CH: But then it gets you to be Grooveshark.

AW: Yeah. You screw up. You fuck up sometimes. But that's the thing. That's the paradox of even why we're having this conversation. Grooveshark got in trouble because it did something wrong, I guess, right, yet millions of people love it, and they consume more music than they ever would have. So where's the balance there? I'm not suggesting

I know what it is, I don't know who does. But I'm suggesting that somewhere in the middle there's got to be something interesting.

We're living in a time where more people have more access to music than at any time in history than they ever have. So you would think, from that perspective, it would be amazing to be a musician, in the same way it's amazing to be a music consumer. So Grooveshark, using that as an example, was a service that tapped into that and doesn't exist. Maybe it should have existed in a different form. Maybe they should have thought about it in a different way. But when you zoom out far enough, the transformation looks like it happens overnight, and when you zoom in really closely, it looks like it happens in lots of fits and starts. Twelve or thirteen years after Napster and we're still talking about these things. And guess what, people have just gone elsewhere, you know? They've just gone to YouTube. They've just gone to other services. They're just playing games.

CH: And I think at the end of the day, the rights holders still have the power, because they control the content. And as you saw with Rdio and Spotify, they got their content licensed, and they are raising money and doing decently, at least Spotify is. But Grooveshark is falling apart and getting sued into oblivion. Are we starting to see a shift away from these startups that need licensed content?

AW: Totally. Rights holders have a power. I wouldn't agree that they have all the power. They have one power. And I don't know anything about the inner workings but from the outside, it appears that those economic arrangements may not be sustainable. They may not be sustainable for the startups, they may not be sustainable for the artists, they may not be sustainable for the rights holders as well. So something is not working. But – the way I think about it is the rights holders hold a power that will allow me to go onto a service like Spotify or Rdio and listen or not listen to a song, but that's just a small bit if you think of the spectrum of power, the importance of that power is decreasing every day. And it decreases every day in a couple of respects – there are other places people go to to find the music, or there are other places that people go to to find something else.

CH: Let's talk about other music startups, like [music collaboration site] Splice, which I know is another recent investment of yours, and SoundCloud. The first time SoundCloud was explained to me, by [USV partner] Fred Wilson, he said it was not a music startup, it was a sound sharing startup. Is that the direction that some people are going to start going in, moving away from these music startups that need all these licenses and need deals with rights holders, and moving toward Splices and SoundClouds and other collaborative tools that allow a little more creative freedom.

AW: Splice and SoundCloud are almost related, in a way. They're almost two sides of the same ecosystem. And the idea behind Splice is – fuck the world of rights. Put those over there. Let's get to the world of how people make music. Let's get to the world of what are the tools that people use to make music. Let's get to the heart of the tools they use to make and share that music, and what if music looked more like software code than .wav files? What would people create if that world existed? And that's the idea of Splice. How can we make it fearless for people to create and share music in many different ways, and if that's the case, many more people will be musicians, because what it means to be a musician is very different. That's completely separate from anything that has to do with rights. Maybe that ends up being more transformational because any person gets to be a musician, because he can program or he can record a really good bassline, a really funky bassline, and on Splice he can take that bassline and let other people use it. And they can iterate it, and they can fork it. So now this person is a musician, but he would never think of himself a musician, and actually in the classical sense of the word he's not really a professional musician, and maybe makes a couple bucks off of it? Nothing to do with rights, or the discussion of rights. It's outside of that world. I don't know, if I was in the music industry, I'd be watching that stuff very closely, because that's the next generation of stuff. And I think that's consistent with the way people are interacting with and manipulating and thinking of media and their media, and thinking of themselves not as passive consumers who just consume but active participants in that consumption and maybe for some of them in the process of what happens to create that consumption. The industry may look very different, but I think your sense of the world is completely accurate.

## Eric Ronning

Sometime in the mid-oughts, I spent a few hours in a rental car futzing with a device that plugged into a cigarette lighter and used an open frequency to play my iPod. I've been in other cars as recently as last year that only had CD players, despite the fact that CD sales have been declining for sixteen years now. The car business simply hasn't kept up with the music biz – although things are starting to change. I spoke to Eric Ronning, EVP and Chief Revenue Officer for Digital at AdLarge Media, about the future of streaming and targeted advertising in cars.

CH: Why have cars been so slow to adopt new technology? We're looking at a state of play now where huge numbers of people have smartphones and iPods, and car manufacturers are just starting to put the connection wires in as a standard. I know this isn't a new problem, because I bought a new car in 2002, and it had a cassette deck. I understand that cars are pretty far behind, but it's getting to the point where it's almost farcical.

ER: You look at the lag time between the technology and something as important to the American people as a car and why they don't match up. But I think what we have to do is think about the reality cycle of the time frame. The purchase cycle of a car is generally seven to ten years. And compare that lifetime to the time it takes to turn over a cell phone being sixteen to eighteen months. So imagine if Apple put out a phone every seven or eight years, and that was the fastest they could upgrade their technology, because that's the time it took you to buy a new one. That alone slows down or makes the perception that it's not happening as fast, but you have to know behind the scenes that those people are working on it diligently, they're thinking about it, and to their credit they have to think about how to put it together in such a way that when the new car is released they haven't just caught up with what has been happening over the past x years, but they're as far ahead into the future as they can get, because this has to last another seven to ten.

CH: Are we starting to see cars coming out now where the technology is in place to plug in your phone? I'll be completely transparent here, I'm a New Yorker and I don't actually own a car, and I haven't purchased a car since 2002. If I was going to buy a new car off the lot tomorrow, what sort of technology would I be looking at?

ER: So most of the new cars now have some sort of digital dashboard that includes the capacity for music or radio, and it's either an auxiliary jack that you can plug into directly or more commonly, now, a Bluetooth connection. And in more cases, and beginning to roll out over the next four to five years, you're beginning to see the in-dash unit which is controlled completely by the car, some of which have their own wireless systems.

CH: I've noticed that when I rent newer cars I get satellite radio and Pandora in dash, and that seems very common – a lot of cars will come with Sirius XM, you get a free year – it's all sort of baked in. So how are they able to break into the car market when a lot of other services haven't been able to?

ER: And if you think about the two companies, they're very different in the way that they've made their way into the car. Starting with Sirius, they started the model years ago. They pay a lot of money to the OEMs, or to the original equipment manufacturers, the car companies. They pay money to the partners to put the radio equipment into the car. When they started it was very low; I think they're up to approximately 60% of the new cars having that system. Whether or not people sign up for it is another thing, but the numbers state that about half of the people who have access to it end up converting to a self-pay subscribership. So they started the model, if you think about that first move, where the radio in your car was always just a feature that had to be in there.

It was just expected, and there was no real upcharge for it, and everybody used it in the same way, and the people who made money on it were largely the radio station selling advertising. And Sirius comes along and creates this new model to disrupt that, and says to the manufacturers, hey, look, we will pay you to be part of that. Change out the units, put in our units, don't get rid of the AM/FM but just put ours in as well so that people have access to it, and to incentivize you we will work with you financially on that process. So that's been a very effective way. They started early enough that their infiltration – and that's benefited by the fact that there's this turnover rate of seven to ten years, right, so they have a lag time before they're completely removed from cars if they were ever to be so. And Pandora is in for, I think, a different kind of reason – they came along at a time of change where people were thinking about online radio, they had proved a model to some degree, they had name brand recognition that it was hard to talk to anybody at the car side or the engineering side or the agency side that was doing advertising – most people, at that point, knew what Pandora was at that time and had a favorable view of its future. They've got that brand recognition, and they certainly have money, and I think their team is up to over thirty people right now that are focused just on in-car systems and those relationships. There's a whole company that just does that. So in the same way that Sirius XM paid or created a financial relationship to get in, I think you can say that Pandora's done a similar thing in that they've put a lot of money into that relationship. They've really taken it very seriously.

CH: The interesting thing about both of those companies, though, is that they're both in-dash. But many people have everything on their phones. Are we going to see any changes based on that?

ER: There's a school of thought that looks at that in the opposite, that the in-dash is just starting to take hold, and you bring your smartphone and tether it either through a cord or through Bluetooth. In 2009, as an example, the percent of Americans that owned a smartphone was about 10%, and the most recent data is showing 2013 that it's up to 53%, so it's about 150 million.

But, of that, demographically, you think about that 53% in 2013, 75% of that number was 18-24, and 75% of 25-34 year olds have their own smart phone, compared to 34% of 55-64 year olds. So that's a prime set of people to reach and to think about. And then you look at some of the actual usage patterns – the #1 thing that people are doing on their smartphones is actually making phone calls. Right? It's like 97%, or more. And then down the line to #10 is listening to online radio, is the 10th thing that they choose to do. But if you break that into heavy use, or daily, the #1 thing that smartphone users is that 91% are making phone calls, and about 18% are listening to online radio on a daily basis. So there's clearly a lot of room for that medium, if you will, of a smartphone to grow, or to be used in that way, and I think that's happening. I think the 2014 data is about to come out soon, and I'm pretty confident you're going to see an uptick in that. I think it's pretty indicative that it's not a done deal.

CH: To dig into the demographics a little bit more, because I thought that was interesting – I grew up driving, and I grew up having a radio on the dash, or putting CDs in the dash, or cassettes in the dash, so I'm a little bit more used to interacting with a dash, whereas if you look at a kid who's just getting their driver's license right now, they might be just so used to interacting with their phone, with their device, that interacting with a dash seems very sort of odd to them. So I wonder if we'll see a shift as the younger kids age up and the people who are used to having in-dash interaction get older. Do you think that's a possibility or is it just too far out?

ER: I think that's a really cool insight, and that group of – that age demographic that you're talking about, that's getting their licenses now or recently, I don't know, even five years ago – those people grew up watching videos in the back seat and playing games with headphones on. And forget listening to online radio or using the dashboard for anything – they weren't even listening to music for the most part.

They were getting their music elsewhere. That was coming from digital sources and other places. It wasn't really associated with the car in the same way I don't think. So the insight there is intriguing. I don't know the answer. I think that's the excitement that everyone is sort of rallying around, is what could be. What is now is certainly not what we're going to end up with, I think everyone agrees with that.

CH: What has the impact of all this been on terrestrial radio? Obviously it's been really seismic, but what are the changes that they're making to survive a little bit longer in this climate?

ER: I think that terrestrial radio stations, or traditional radio broadcast groups, are certainly healthy, and they've been working very hard in the last ten years to think about what they do next. I think content is going to be the key deciding factor for a lot of these choices. I think it's going to be experiential. And terrestrial has some really good experience in programming and how to put those things together, so that's not a lost scenario at all. They're experimenting with multi-channels, so the programming directors of these radio stations are creating pure online radio stations, with visions of their own passion, the music that they'd put together if they didn't have to be constrained by lowest common denominator on the radio signal, and those things are available through digital and HD radio or also streaming. So there's things of that nature.

But generally speaking, what seems to be happening is the radio side of the house, or those with experience in traditional radio, seem to be favoring the concept of live and local. I think the meaning behind that has been largely talent, the sound and voice, the feel of the radio station, the information that you gather, the locality of that being a, to quote the old kind of thinking, the friend that's in your car. I think they're trying to figure out how to take that advantage and go the next step. The difficulty for traditional radio has been in many situations, the large ownership groups have kind of diminished their own value there, because they've gone to voice tracking and a national syndicated model where one DJ voice is in 20 cities and gets some kind of overlay to make it feel like he's in that city or she's in that city. So you kind of have to think about that. It's unclear. There's certainly a large footprint, there's certainly a favored nation usage for the demographics, I think this younger group that's coming up and going forward will be very telling. The radio industry puts out a lot of data that says that younger audience is still using radio and that their time with audio consumption has increased because of these other options, and those in the pure play market are favoring reports that say, contrary to that, that they're not using much traditional radio and that they're seeking their information elsewhere. I tend to believe, as usual, that the truth probably lies somewhere in the middle of all that. It's going to be up for grabs, for the best experience is going to win, the best presentation and marketing of who you are to the user is going to win. Pandora has won the early rounds in this because the word of mouth was excellent.

In the early days it was the engineers passing it off to other people in their office, and then those people passing it off to their friends, and then those people pass it to their parents, and that's really hard to replicate. I don't think that can be replicated again.

CH: I think another big, big differentiator between terrestrial radio and streaming is that people have really different expectations to the number of ads that they'll put up with. On the rare occasion that I do listen to commercial terrestrial radio, because I'm not in a car that often, I'm shocked by how many ads there are. I'm completely blown away by how much time is taken up by ads, as opposed to streaming, where I just pay $10/month for Spotify, and I'm like "Hey, no ads, great,", but if I'm listening to Pandora, which I don't pay for, it's a couple ads an hour, if that. So how is this all going to play out? Is terrestrial going to have to cut back? Is streaming going to start playing more to make up for it? What's the future for this conflict?

ER: Well, I don't think it's been resolved yet, by any stretch, but I think it's fair to say that the concept of people accepting more ads on terrestrial than they would on pure play is not real. I don't think anybody will accept a large number of ads if they don't have to. So, you know, that level of – "Hey, we've always been able to run 18 minutes an hour so that's going to go on forever," I mean, that's just not realistic by any stretch of the imagination.

This concept of spot load following the radio clock, or the timing, the programming clock, or when you hit music, when you get news and information, when you get your commercial breaks – I think that's probably pretty outdated based on what you can do today, but it's hard to change that in the terrestrial space for a couple of reasons. The competitive set pretty much demands that, as much as everybody who's a programmer or owner would love to run way less commercials and charge more for them, it's a really difficult move to make. And it's difficult because the people who pay the money for it don't want to pay more money, and the people who own or invest in the radio holding groups don't want to make less money. And there's always a human element. You've got to make the number, so even with the best intentions, if a radio station cuts back their station load and says "We're only going to take 5 units an hour, we're going to charge more because they're worth more now," it's very noble, and it usually lasts a little while, but the competitors find a way to get the business, and that company, quite often, will change their tune. Whereas terrestrial is kind of locked into that – so I think it's going to be harder for them to make a shift. Pure play, on the other hand, they came out of the box with the expectation of no commercials. I think a lot of these music companies were built by people who were dissatisfied with the music that they could get in traditional radio, and they wanted a better answer, and that better answer to them was "I don't want any commercials." So there's a lot of zealotry at that level, with these companies that were built with, you know, "Let's create music that is always accessible, no commercialization, it'll be great," and then the reality of – you know, they get investors who want to make money.

CH: Yeah, exactly. It's all fun and games until you have to pay your employees, or until you have to pay your rights holders.

ER: So that reality sets in, and I think most of these companies have matured to the point where they clearly get it. I think Pandora's a good example. When they started out that was their story, and they very wisely and professionally moved to a model which seems to work for them, which is not that many ads, a good price that's fair to both parties, and still keeps a good user engagement going.

CH: I wanted to touch on another key differentiator with ads on streaming vs. ads on terrestrial, which is the microtargeting. Let's say you're a radio station in New York, obviously people buy ads for the New York market. Well, the New York market is massive. So if I'm in my car in Brooklyn and I hear an ad for something in the Bronx, that's irrelevant to me. But from everything that I've read, the trend now for the streaming services is to microtarget, and to microtarget down to pretty much your exact location. So if I'm in my car in Greenpoint, Brooklyn, I'm going to hear an ad for a business that's in Greenpoint, Brooklyn, and I'm going to also hear an ad that is catered to the fact that I'm a woman in my 30s driving a Zipcar, a Prius, all this different data that they can get from me. So I'd just like to hear what that's going to look like in 5 to 10 years, and how terrestrial going to survive *that*.

ER: It's an interesting problem, and I think if you look at and go back just a touch. Let's start with the traditional radio, right? Typically between $16 billion and $20 billion/year have traded hands in advertising for terrestrial radio stations, which are transmitter by radio towers in a field that can project their frequency about 60 miles in any direction, plus or minus. So locality was just not something you thought about. It was a given. Chicago station, it had to be in Chicago. New York station, it had to be in New York. Couldn't hear it in San Francisco, except a couple of Clear Channel AMs. So that concept built that $16-20 billion business. And it was largely based on large national brand advertisers that are everywhere and wanted to reach people through this medium, and medium to large local advertisers who were relatively ubiquitous, like a J&R or something like that, who are in many locations but who are specific to a city, and it didn't really help the small business, the one-shop owners, the people who were trying to grow. It really wasn't too practical to invest your money in traditional radio until you had a certain size. It was hard. The promise of the digital audio is this microtargeting that you speak of, which is real. The technical capacity to do that exists. It is not, by any stretch of the imagination, as perfect as many of the owners, or people with vested interest in that technology, would have us believe, but is certainly available and possible. Much of that information is based on multiple sources that are stitched together either through partnerships or through simple access that – you go scrape the info. And any time you're cobbling stuff together like that, there's weakness in the chain, and there's potential for mismatching. So the only way to know that you're a woman in a Prius in Brooklyn is through a combination of some geolocation connectivity, that they're GPS tracking you, and that you are in the car because that information is somehow connected to the car, so it knows it's that car, and that has to be linked together somehow, and that you're a woman because they've either implied it by what you're listening to, which is a weak way to go, but the way that it's been done – or that there's some registration data for that car or for that GPS device that's associated with you. So getting all of that info from one source is really the sticky wicket.

And there are multiple ways to share that information, and cross that information over, and assume things, and capture it, and – it just – it's not there yet. So a company like Pandora has the greatest potential because they have as close to a closed loop system for listenership and relationship with each user as you can get. You register, you give them information about you, you listen, you repeat, and you can be tracked by – it's your cell phone that you're listening to, or they have some idea of where you are physically. Conversely, for ad networks, or people who are putting together multiple partners, that's a much more difficult task, because if you're not Pandora, or *maybe* Clear Channel, it's very difficult to get your user group to offer up registration data. It's certainly difficult to get realistic registration data. That's one of the fascinating things about Pandora; you ask them and talk to people their, they'll share with you – their registration data is about as pure as you can get in the online space. People don't lie about who they are when they sign up for Pandora.

 That's the interesting thing about music, and this relationship with audio via terrestrial or pure play. There's a real connection there, that is, I think, something we don't fully understand on the advertising side, its importance. You're connected to music so deeply and so personally. If you look at Facebook, and you look at who you project as a person, you have probably, like most people, embellished some part of that to shine up your person, or your presentation of self, for the public.

CH: Oh, yeah, absolutely. Everyone does.

ER: But you probably, as is in almost every case, did nothing at all except share exactly who you are musically in that same process. Right?

CH: I work in the music industry, so probably there's a few bands I list as bands that I like because they're cool, even though I probably don't listen to them that often, but –

ER: But if they came on you wouldn't turn them off.

CH: Probably not. And I'm probably more of an outlier because I do have to – because I work in the music industry. I feel like most normal people will just list stuff that they like and call it a day.

ER: If you can put together a way to say, "Ok, this musical taste, or this musical direction, is more indicative of who this person is in their heart and soul than what they've told me about what they like, long walks on the beach and blah blah blah," that's a missed part of the growth here that I think is going to catch on now that we're connected digitally, now that we're thinking about what we can glean or find or intuit or whatever you want to do through that, and I think that's probably going to be the power of what this audio connection is going to be in the future, I think that's everything.

CH: When I do listen to the radio in the car, a lot of the time it's to hear the traffic report. People want to hear the weather on the ones, or the traffic on the fives, or the top headlines of the day or whatever. And they're not really paying as much attention to the other stuff on the radio, they just want to know "Should I bring my umbrella?" or "Should I take this road or that road?" So, you know, that's something that streaming services can't offer right now. You can listen to Pandora and hear great music, but you can't listen to Pandora and hear a traffic report. So I'm wondering if there's some way integrates, so that you can get Google Traffic integrated into your Spotify stream, so every five songs your Google Traffic report will come on, and because you're in a connected car – again, if I'm driving in Brooklyn, I don't really care that there's an accident in New Jersey. I want to know if the BQE has problems or construction. And because I'm using Google Maps, you know, I've entered my destination. So if I'm driving from Brooklyn to Long Island, it's going to tell me if there's a problem on the Long Island Expressway, it's not going to bother me with, like "Oh, there's something in New Jersey or Connecticut that seems troubling." I'm just sort of wondering what that future looks like.

ER: Refer back to the conversation about terrestrial thinking about themselves as live and local. That's the advantage. That's what they've done, that's part of the content, that's what they consider to be radio. That's part of the experience. And the news, the weather, the local information, the bands playing, the local gossip, the local politics, all of that, is all part of quote-unquote "the show". So I do believe that's a huge advantage for terrestrial currently, and I do see that the streaming services that you would consider pure plays have not necessarily woven that into their experiences, currently. I think a lot of that has been growth and learning from the pure play ownerships, who, you know, remember, these companies largely started as some really smart tech engineer people who put this stuff together out of love, and it just kind of grew, and it's only recently that traditional radio thinking has integrated itself into those models, that they've hired people from that other side and they're starting to share information. So you've gotta believe that they're aware of it, and that technologically it's not impossible to drop that kind of information that's self-selected into your programming. There was a guy at CBS, David Goodman, who I work with, and he had an idea a while ago that is still relevant, that was the pick and choose format, that you pick your format, you pick your DJ, you can your news source, you pick your sports source, and you put it all together as your own self-serve custom radio station top to bottom. And I don't think that's unthought of concept, I think that's out there in multiple areas, I think people have thought about it and looked at it. I think technologically it can be done. I think the will to do it is, you know, it's hard for people to make that leap.

CH: We've heard about how millennials don't consume ads in the same way that people like you or I do. We grew up before DVRs, and before being able to skip ads, and before being able to watch whatever you want whenever you want on your iPad, and while I don't have a huge tolerance for sitting through ads, my tolerance for sitting through ads is much more than a 20-year-old's or a 10-year-old's would be. For kids, a thirty second ads for a product is weird and old and disruptive, but they're totally fine with Chris Brown writing a song about Wrigley's Gum and it becoming a hit. These are kids that would never look at a billboard, but they'll follow the Denny's Tumblr. So how are advertisers going to deal with that, especially on streaming services, and in terrestrial, too – you know, you're dealing with a post-ad generation. What do they do? What's the next step?

ER: Well, I think this is the idea of native advertising, which is a bandied-about phrase that is important now, I guess, people are talking about that. And I guess it's easy to understand what native advertising is in print or a website content, integrated into an editorial, integrated into the content in a way that feels as – part of the show.

And that concept of placed advertising has been around for ages. There are firms in Los Angeles that – that was their business, was creating those connections and getting product placement in movies, TV, etc. etc. So that's not a new thing. And that's what cracks me up about this new concept of native advertising, it's exactly what's always happened.

CH: Yeah. But how do you do that in radio? That's my big question – it's easy – well, not easy, but possible – to do it on TV, it's doable in print and on the web, how in the world do you do native advertising on radio?

ER: I don't think it's clear yet. I think podcasting has some great ideas for that, because it acts the most like a show that you can integrate content into, because it's spoken word that you're listening to, and that's the most natural way to do it. I think you can look back to Howard Stern, who is clearly, in my view, just the master of doing that. He was able to integrate his sponsors into his show in a way that was completely natural and made sense for who he was and who his audience is. Right? You know, you can't get any more perfect than that. What the media's missing today is that kind of personality with that kind of power, or the willingness to use personalities in that way. I think we're getting there, I think you're going to start to find this balance that seems right. And, I think, using the Howard Stern example again, as far as I know, to a fault, I think every sponsor he actually took on was someone he believed in and cared about. So, you know, it was coming from the heart in some way, shape or form – he was connected to it. He found a piece of it that made it real, and that's natural. That's native. You can't just pay someone to say stuff.

CH: But how do you integrate that into music? That's great for Howard Stern, that's great for talk radio –

ER: So I hope your Chris Brown example is not the long-term future, because that would make me sad as a person who likes music –

CH: Yeah, me too.

ER: But it's possible. I guess, the changing idea of artists and who they are, that's altering.

CH: Right.

ER: That association and value is huge. Artists are much more aware of the value that they have in that process, and there are much more people in businesses helping them extract that value for their brand. So I think that's going to continue, no question about it. But on the more basic level, for the local advertisers, or the medium advertisers that cannot actually afford to have a deal with Beyonce or have her write a song for you, how do you do that? And I can't help but go back to the associative value of the experience itself, should be a really valuable thing. If you feel good about the music you're listening to, or call a station that you're listening to, or your selection of music that you've been involved in and feel personally associated with, and there's a proper alignment of an advertiser that makes sense for you in that kind of right way, and I don't think that's a 60-second ad, or a 30-second ad that's terrestrial that's kind of moved over online, I think it has to be crafted for the experience, I think that can be very successful. I've had some experience with that with my business partner at the time, Andy Lipset and I, when we did Ronning Lipset Radio, we did a lot of experimenting with clients to that nature. We did custom ads for online that spoke to the fact that they knew people were listening online – I think they resonated. It was very simple. We're not marketing geniuses. So somebody who really cares to dig into it and who can do it well, I think it can be very powerful.

CH: Looking at the post-ad world, people never had to pay for terrestrial radio, obviously, it was just something you could turn on and listen to, and that was part of what was great about it, it was so accessible. But now people are being offered the chance to pay for the streaming services and not listen to the ads, and the price point is, I would say, for the most part, pretty compelling. It's $10/month for Spotify, it's pretty cheap for Pandora, these are all great deals. And people are comfortable paying for Netflix, paying for Hulu, you know, they kinda get this. Do you think this will ever reach a mass adoption, where it's just part of their cable bill, it's part of their monthly expenses, and then what happens to the advertisers if that's the case, because they're kind of locked out? Do we, again, see this kind of Chris Brown-esque future where pop songs are secretly about soda pop or chewing gum, or what do we see advertisers do? What's the solution for radio?

ER: I don't know that we know yet. I think historically, leading up to today, as much as the recent insights or data shows, you can see – there's really been nobody who's been able to break 5% of an audience, 10%, something of that nature, you can't get much more than that to pay for music that's commercial-free. So you see subscription models, it's certainly something that investors like because it's an annuity, you can count it up, you can tell how much in conversion rates – if I do this, if I get this many people, I make this much money – but there's a limit to the number, the size of the audience that you can garner that way. In almost every case, people who have started off as pure subscription model have somehow managed to find a free model as well to augment that.

**Ben Sisario**

A few years ago, I chatted with Ben Sisario, who reports on the changing landscape of the music industry for the New York Times. I talked with Ben about how YouTube's plans for a music awards show and a subscription music service might impact the online music sector, why streaming music services more broadly haven't gained a foothold in the larger market, and the Miley Cyrus outrage cycle.

CH: Tell me about your writing process and how it plays out for you and your role at the New York Times.

BS: Well, I have editors, and I have a lot of them. And they change stuff. I mean, I guess on some basic level it's not a lot different from people who write for other publications in that I have my sources, and I pitch my editors, and we fight about things, and then things run, and then people yell at me for them. But I think that I have two distinct constituencies that I'm writing for, and that I have to think about, and one is the music industry and people who are very knowledgeable about the things that I'm writing about, and then the other is the general reader, who probably doesn't know, or you have to assume doesn't know a great deal of detail about the topics, and may know nothing. It can be a trick, sometimes, to figure out what story's appropriate or what story's not appropriate, what's too in the weeds versus what's actually a revealing detail about the way an industry works and the way it impacts normal people. So, I mean, that's one thing that often comes up between me and my editors – is this inside baseball or not? And sometimes we disagree about that, but I think that's generally kind of the challenge.

CH: What's your solution? Do you say "I'm going to do 50% in-the-weeds industry stories and 50% broader interest stories?"

BS: That's not the way I look at it. I mean, I try to make every story comprehensible and meaningful, and, you know, sometimes it's inevitably in the weeds, but you try to write that lede in a way that explains it. Especially as the digital music industry has developed, and the issues that are demanding the most attention now, they're very much in the weeds – royalties, and a lot of the legal issues about rights and copyright and downloads and streaming and whatever, this is really complicated stuff – so you can't dismiss it as, just, you know – Spotify and all the stuff about who gets paid, and YouTube and who gets paid, and the rights – that's not just minutiae that nobody cares about. In a way it's minutiae, but it's minutiae that is very meaningful and that impacts everything. So, this is a conversation that I wind up having with my editors a lot, where I'll say something like, "Hey, this is going on, this is a big deal," and you'll kind of get the glassy-eyed response, of, you know, talking about mechanical royalties. And you then you've gotta sort of go "Ok, this person doesn't spend their whole day reading Billboard and talking with publishing sources or whatever," and so you have to think about the reader that doesn't know all of the industry detail. And so I actually think it's a really useful exercise all the time, is just to take a really difficult subject and a subject that is not known by everybody and try to explain it, and I think it's the same thing that a lot of reporters here have to deal with, if you're covering health care, or the tax code, or something. Like when a thousand-page tax bill is pushed through Congress at the last minute, it has to be explained to people in 900 words, just like anything else, and so you have to figure out – what is the key point, what are the disagreements, and what does it mean?

CH: Let's shift gears and talk about someone very mainstream, who probably doesn't need much explaining – Miley Cyrus. To me, Miley, with the twerking and the tongue and the this and the that, it's clear that she's just trolling people. It's clear that she's a very intelligent young woman who grew up in the music industry, learned it at her father's knee, she's the one sitting there with her team of social media experts planning this stuff out, and yet people are still really outraged by it. They're still clutching at their pearls. And no one seems to have figured out that this is all manufactured outrage, that this is all just made up, and that this is all just people jumping on a bandwagon to drive pageviews and hits and Spotify streams. I'm kind of curious as to why you think that people can't really – there's this appetite for coverage of someone like Miley Cyrus, but people can't figure out that it's all sort of made up to get attention, as opposed to anything real.

BS: As opposed to anything real. I don't know. I guess – I don't really want to defend Miley Cyrus coverage, because I hate it, I feel like it's a non-story, and I'm tired of reading about it. I think that it's depressing, you know, media perpetuates itself, and perpetuates a story like this, because I think you're right, there's the – the pageview trolling clickbait kind of aspect to it that we just see over and over and over again. So I don't know. We've seen it happen before, we know exactly what's going on, and by we I mean people in the music industry who knows what's going on or people who are just savvy consumers of media. I do think, though, that the average consumer – I don't know what they think about a star, a performer doing something outrageous for the sake of publicity versus doing something outrageous for some other reason. And in the case of Kanye West or something –what's the difference? His whole approach to his art, and to his persona, is about exploring the absurd side of celebrity and just going crazy with it, and I think maybe there's a sexist side to it, but I think we look at Kanye West as someone who's going about it in a sort of savvy way. And there's a sort of ingenious musical side to him, but he's also making troll-like tweets all the time. And, like, grabbing a mic away from Taylor Swift, which is just as stupid. I don't think I have a great answer to your question. Like you, I think it sucks, it's not interesting, but it's also kind of interesting to just watch media happen.

CH: I have this theory that it's a ten-year, give-or-take, outrage cycle. Because when I was a kid, the Madonna Sex book was the big thing, and when I was in college it was Britney and Christina Aguilera in their tiny little outfits, and now it's Miley Cyrus, and I was thinking – is there a ten-year window that most normal people have where they really care about pop culture, and then they sort of grow out of it and forget it? This constant newness of – oh, another naked pop star, because they have no memory of the naked pop star ten years earlier?

BS: I like theories like that.

CH: Ok.

BS: I go with it. But do you think that there hasn't been outrage about exhibitionistic celebrities in the last ten years?

CH: Oh, yeah, there's always - I mean, it goes back to Elvis. I just think people have a very short memory span.

BS: But there's been nothing from Britney to Miley?

CH: Nothing that I feel like has been as big, in terms of naked female pop stars.

BS: What about Lady Gaga and the meat dress?

CH: Gaga and the meat dress was a little different, though. Britney's nakedness and Miley's almost nakedness were treated in this almost sort of patronizing way, whereas Gaga and the meat dress was just like "Oh, she's quirky, she's a different duck."

BS: Yeah.

CH: It was a little bit more respectful. Lady Gaga can and does walk around very scantily clad, but because she handles herself differently people just think, like, she's a weirdo, but it's not – she's the least sexualized naked woman in pop music these days, if that makes any sense, which is not an insult. But she's operating on a completely different level. Yeah, there's probably been other naked pop star scandals that I've missed, but these sort of seem to be the big tent-pole – haha – naked pop star lady scandals.

BS: This is Cortney's first book in the making.

CH: Yes.

BS: Maybe it's me showing my age, but I just – I felt, and did you read Camille Paglia's piece about Miley Cyrus? She wrote about it.

CH: Yes, and I wanted to jump off a bridge after I read it.

BS: I agreed with her that I thought that there was – it wasn't so much that there was a sexual norm that was being flouted, or that was shocking the world, as much as I just thought it was a really lame performance. I find it hard to believe that people turning on the television in 2013 would go: "[gasp] A girl shaking her ass? *What?!*" How will my children possibly survive? But it just was ridiculous. It was terrible. That's what was outrageous to me.

CH: Yeah. She's not a very good dancer. I'll concede that point. She's a lot of things, and god knows she'll be running a record label in 20 years, but she's not a dancer, that one.

BS: Whatever happened, it did the trick, you're right. The end result is popularity, is eyeballs, is clicks, is people hitting the button. And that's – that's what it's about. That's pop, that's the purpose. So I guess on a simplistic level, like Elvis, it got people to pay attention.

CH: I want to ask about streaming music.. Everyone I know in New York, LA and San Francisco has either Spotify or Rdio. People have their preferences, but everyone in my immediate circle has one or the other. But no one I know outside of those major media centers does,especially older people, so people over 35 or 40 definitely don't.  I'm kind of curious as to why it hasn't caught on in a meaningful way outside of a small population – is it a failure in marketing, which is my personal theory, or is it just that these services are too early, in 10 years they'll be the norm, it just takes a while – why do you not think Spotify and Rdio haven't become the default for most people?

BS: I guess marketing has a role, but my own theory is that the product just isn't good enough. I think that, at this point, it's been a decade. It's been more than a decade that there's been the streaming model. And I think that there – for people who are huge consumers of music, things like Spotify are – they're useful resources, and they're – it's kind of the dream of the celestial jukebox, of "type in the name and it pops up" – but I believe, speaking as a consumer, that they're just not fun places to spend time, that they're just not that appealing as destinations. I think iTunes actually kind of was – I think it's – I guess it had the advantage of being the only big one for a while, but its slickness was a big benefit. And I think, as much as I – I use Spotify all the time, I use Rdio all the time, and I try as many of the others as I can, just to keep familiar with everything, but I just don't find myself all that dazzled with the interface.

CH: And where does something like Muve Music come in? Muve is part of the Cricket Wireless network, and it has this huge audience. Almost no one ever covers it. It's not included in the same conversations as Spotify or Rdio, and I think that's at least partially because their subscriber base is not affluent. Cricket Wireless is pay-as-you-go cell phone, which is generally targeted at any audience that doesn't have a lot of money or good credit, so where does something like that fit into this broader picture of streaming services?

BS: Good question. You're exactly right about Muve Music and Cricket, and they specifically target that segment of the market, and I think that's a really savvy idea. And they've been successful. But I don't know – I don't have an answer of what it says for the whole picture. I guess it does challenge the whole idea of – it's only affluent young media-drunk people who are signing up for this. There are all kinds of other people out there who will do it if it does what – if the service does what they want it to do. And Muve Music, I guess, does what they need it to do. The people behind Muve would – they would often say that their consumer only has a phone. They do not have a computer, they do not have a tablet, and the phone is everything. And the simplicity of the service is what appeals to their customer. And so it's – download the song, pay a fairly small amount in addition to your carrier cost – and by the way, maybe that's a big part of it, is that they've done bundling. They've done it. And bundling has been a real issue for most of the other digital services. They haven't really been able to bag the big providers, the big telecom companies. And once that happens maybe that will change things, if it happens.


CH: YouTube announced that they're going to be hosting a music awards show, and a lot of publications have suggested that the timing of the music awards show and the timing of the subscription service are not a coincidence. Is this YouTube trying to reposition itself away from being this chaotic place where if you – if I search for any given song I'll get the official video and I'll get a hundred videos of someone's baby dancing to it or dog doing something cute to it, or some kid playing a cover song in his basement? What's YouTube really trying to do with this awards show?

BS: I think that they are sort of trying to reposition themselves, but I think YouTube wants to be the chaotic place for the wedding video and the dog on the skateboard as well as the moneymaking video, and so far their attempt to do that with the channels that they launched at the beginning of the year has not been a resounding success.

CH: Oh, god, I'd forgotten about that until right now.

BS: Yeah, that's a big deal. And that was a strategy at the very top of YouTube, maybe Google too, of what is YouTube all about, how are we going to make money on this and pitch this to people so they can make money too, and the result, I think, is that – yeah, a lot of the people who have put the official channels on there are getting the views, but I think it's more the viral effect. Whether it's on an official channel doesn't really matter. It's still just sometimes there's a spark and it lights something on fire and it just happens. So, I don't know. I think YouTube is trying to juggle a lot right now, and, again, they're powerful, maybe they'll be able to do it, but maybe what people want out of YouTube is different from what YouTube wants to be.

# David McMillin

Indie musician David McMillin wrote a great essay on PopMatters called "Why It's Time to Stop Hating Spotify," and I knew I had to have a longer conversation with him. In the piece, McMillin adds an indie musician's perspective to the royalty payout discussion, and floats the idea that maybe Spotify isn't run by a bunch of sadists. I talked to the Fort Frances frontman about his essay, Spotify music royalties, Tidal, and much more.

CH: Let's dive right in and start talking about this piece on PopMatters that you wrote about Spotify. You pushed back against this notion that the company is paying artists in essentially rolls of pennies. I'd love to talk to you about what inspired you to write this piece and join this sort of larger ongoing discussion.

DM: First off, thanks for reading it and continuing the discussion. You know, it's something that I talk about it with plenty of people in the music business, but I also talk about it with plenty of people that are just music fans. You know, maybe they use Spotify, maybe they still download music – however they actually consume their media. And honestly – there aren't a ton of topics where I want to sit down and craft a well-written essay, but I wanted to take some time with this one, because I think the discussion has been one-sided. I wanted to kind of offer a little bit of a more balanced perspective. I think Spotify does get a bad rap. Would it be great if everyone was making *more* money from it? I couldn't argue with that. But I think the notion that people aren't making any money at all, and that it's destroying the music business, is something that's also untrue.

CH: People have suggested that blame be shifted away from the streaming services and more onto the labels in terms of the low artist payouts. Spotify and other services do, in fact, pay the labels, and then the labels are responsible for paying the artists. Do you think there's some validity to that statement -  that people should be looking at the labels and not just the streaming services?

DM: Yeah, I definitely do. I'd imagine you guys saw there was a contract with Sony leaked, I think, two weeks ago, I honestly haven't had time to read the whole thing, it's a pretty long contract. I do think people should be looking at the labels in the larger conversation. There are a lot of middlemen in the music business. And while I say I think people should be looking at the labels I also would say that I think one of the big pieces that I personally think is that I'm not trying to take the stance that everyone should be independent. To be really transparent, my band has been doing everything independently for so long, and we'd love the marketing muscle and resources that a good record label can offer. I think the thing to keep in mind is that a number of major label artists, and I reference Portishead in my article, have complained about the payout that they receive from streaming services, but that is more indicative of the contracts that they have found themselves in. So I do think it's important to just bring awareness to the fact that Spotify isn't the one in charge of paying out everyone. In many cases there are other people in charge of collecting the revenue.

CH:  I feel like many of these bands – you know, Portishead, and some of the others that I've sort of thought about – they signed their major label contracts twenty years ago.

DM: Exactly.

CH: And any sort of digital clause in there – they signed contracts that don't reflect the reality today, and I feel like that's a huge part of it. Obviously you can't predict the future, but they do have to take a little bit of responsibility for signing these deals presumably in good faith.

DM: I certainly agree there.  I think that musicians and many people kind of, just involved in the music business in general, we're all kind of guilty of thinking of revenue and potential to make money off of creative work in a very siloed approach. It's like, you make x amount of dollars from streaming, you make x amount of dollars from downloads, you make x amount of money from touring, and from licensing, and sync. I think it's important, particularly on the major label side, well, actually, really across the board, to think of those as a very holistic approach. To think that Portishead may have made a smaller chunk of change from their streaming services, but they are also making a *lot* of money from playing live, from basically having access to the opportunities that a label has helped them get. So, you know, it's a two-way street.

CH: At the end of the day, you are selling your talent to the people who want to pay for it. And that's not a bad thing, that's just the reality of the new economy is that you don't have a sort of siloed career anymore. You don't have this sort of x number of record sales, x number of ticket sales sort of thing. You know, you still get separate checks, but part of it is like – what is the market willing to bear, and who's willing to pay for it? I saw Portishead headline All Tomorrow's Parties in Iceland last year, and it was incredible.

DM: Oh, nice.

CH: Yeah, it was an incredible show. They're a fantastic band. But they're a very nineties band. You know, I don't know they would have had as many young people watching them play were they not on streaming services.

DM: That's a great point.

CH: Now there are other revenue streams, and I'm not just talking about, oh, you can sell your music to a TV commercial, though that's a new stream. There are so many other branding opportunities, and people that are willing to pay for you to be part of their community, or endorse their brand. I've seen bands sell crazy associated merchandise.

Let's say you have a really cool style, you have a really unique take on how you look, you could put up a really great Pinterest page for your band, and everything you wear you could sell, and you could cut a deal with a clothing company, and that's something that didn't exist twenty years ago. I mean, Beth from Portishead's very attractive and stylish, and I don't know that she would personally do this, but potentially that's another revenue stream for her.

DM: The music business is continuing to evolve. But what you're getting at is the crux of what will be the future of the music business, and that's having bands that are really really hungry to be successful, and to diversify how they make enough money to be a successful touring and performing band. Like it or not, just not as many people download and buy music anymore. But it's still clear that people still need and want music in their lives. So as a band it's just about how you take what you're doing and monetize it in a new way. And yeah, I mean – we can – many people might call someone like me talking about what kind of branding partnerships you can work on, you could call that a sellout, but I call that reality.

CH: Ian MacKaye, the lead singer of Fugazi, was at an event I was at, and somebody asked him about it. And he is one of the arbiters of that? And he was like "Look, man, however you pay your rent, that's how you pay your rent." He's like "I personally wouldn't sell my song to a soda company, but I wouldn't judge anyone." It's like – do what you gotta do. And I see a very big age divide in terms of the critics of streaming music. I'm setting aside Taylor Swift for a minute. Even though she's young, she's still had sort of an old school music business career – everyone else that I can think of that's very vocal about hating streaming is older. They're Gen X, they're not even boomers so much, although I guess there is AC/DC. A lot of them are of a specific demographic. And I feel like some of it is that younger people and younger artists have grown up with this new reality, and they're much more comfortable with this, whereas older artists, who are kind of a little bit entitled, like "We're gonna sell a bunch of CDs!" "We're gonna go out on tour and compete with musicians with other countries and musicians who play other types of music!" You know, they felt sort of like, "Oh, I'm a dude in an indie band, I can just go do this thing." They are really freaked out by this. Because you're not entitled to that any more.

DM: No, no. And, you know, this is kind of an aside, it's a funny story. Even aside from the critics who play music, I think it's really important to talk about just the end listener – who's using it. I'm still baffled by the fact that Spotify only has 60 million users and 15 million are paid. I love Spotify as a listener, as someone who likes to discover music, you know. So I sent that PopMatters article to my dad, I mean, he's like 64, I think? My folks have been big champions of, you know, they're supportive of a son who plays music, anyway, but – they read it and they were like "So, you had 284,000 streams, so theoretically, that – you know, a decade ago, you would have sold 284,000 albums," and I was like "No."

It doesn't really work that way. I'm blown away by the fact that our band has, you know, 280-some thousand streams and growing and will continue to grow. We are reaching new audiences that never, ever would have heard us. If you're talking even five years ago, these people never would have found us. If you're talking the ease of discovery, and this is specific to Spotify because I use it but I think a lot of streaming services are, you know, they're getting pretty good at this, at just making discovery a more fun experience, and better. If you listen to Band A, you find Band B who you never would have listened to before, but you're into them. Let's say you stream their song 100 times. Well, that's better than streaming them no times and never ever considering going to a show or following them on Twitter and getting to know more about them. I just feel that streaming is creating a lot more opportunities than it is killing revenue.

CH: I'm not surprised that Spotify has so relatively few users – I mean, 50 million is still a lot, but that doesn't surprise me. Because if you look at the numbers from the late '90s, which I think most people agree was the height of the modern music business, you know, the N'Sync era, the average person still spent like $50 a year roughly on music.

DM: Really, it's that low? Wow.

CH: Yeah, so what you had was an audience that was very front-loaded, that was spending a lot of money on music. Right? You had to spend a lot of money on music. You had to. I mean, I would spend $18 on a CD in the late '90s, because that was the only way I could get music.

DM: Totally.

CH: You had an audience of passionate music fans who were overspending, they were spending hundreds and hundreds of dollars a year, but then the long tail was sort of your average Joe or Jane who liked music well enough, and bought three or four CDs a year, and listened to the radio. Now, the problem is you still have your average Joe or Jane who buys three or four CDs a year, and Spotify's not really a good deal for them because they're spending less money buying stuff on iTunes or buying CDs than they would subscribing to Spotify. So they look at the $120 a year as opposed to the $50 a year that they're spending, and they're like "Well, that's dumb." But then what's happened is that you have people like me who were spending hundreds of dollars a year spend $120 a year. And I'm sure you're the same way. You probably spent a ton of money on music, now you have Spotify, and you're like "Oh, well, I don't have to" – you're still paying for music, it's still good. They've essentially gotten rid of the higher spenders without bringing on the lower spenders. The other thing that streaming services do really well is for bands like you, it allows people to just sort of check stuff out.

DM: Totally.

CH: It was very hard to just check out a song prior to the middle of last decade, before the rise of YouTube. People would tell me to check out a band, and I was like, OK, I have to remember the name of that band, go to the record store, maybe listen to it on headphones standing in the middle of the record store?

DM: Listening stations, yeah.

CH: Not the greatest way to experience music. And then I have to commit $14 or $16 to purchasing this thing which I may or may not actually like. So a lot of bands – probably just no-one ever bothered to check 'em out. Now I get emails and tweets all day long with like "Check this out, check this out" – and my worst-case scenario is that I lose a few minutes of my time.

DM: People need music now more than ever, and it's clear they do. Look at the health of the festival market. People are spending loads of money on massive festivals. The festival market wasn't nearly what it was ten years ago. I mean, think about the cool experiences that those festivals are offering. Back to your point on just selling cool merch – it's just not as simple anymore as making a record and hoping that people buy it and maybe they see you play.

CH: I feel like there's been a huge shift in the way that we consume. For a long time, people were, generally, product consumers, so you showed off your success with the fact that you had a nice house, or you had two cars, or you had a Gucci purse...You had physical products, and CDs and records were physical products. I remember, in high school, going over to people's houses, and they had walls of CDs, and just being like "Oh, this is so cool. Oh, I want to live here someday."

DM: CD towers.

CH: I feel like with the rise of this sort of social media, people have really shifted away, for the most part, from this sort of product economy to the experience economy. Because now you can share your experiences globally. Pre-social media, you could only share your experiences with the people that were physically around you so it made more sense to have tons of stuff 'cause that was, like, how you marked your success. Well, now you can throw your photo up on Instagram of you, like, "I'm at the Taj Mahal," or "I'm skiing in Aspen," or "I'm at the cool festival," and those experiences are now the new social currency. So it kind of makes sense in music with the rise of festivals. The Onion put out a funny story that was like "New music festival is just a field for people to do drugs in." I remember asking someone at some big music festival "Oh, who are you excited to see?" And he said "I dunno. I'm just here." And it wasn't even like "Oh, I'm just here to check out new bands, or discover new stuff." It was like "I don't know, my friends came, I came, just drinking beer." A lot of festivals, they have great music, but the music almost feels secondary – especially Coachella, Coachella's like a fashion show with a bunch of bands.

DM: I live in Chicago. I only go to the Lollapalooza aftershows. They're only $20, and you end up seeing the bands I would have wanted to see but didn't want to go at 3 o'clock to see. Basically, the festival is just a fashion runway.

CH: Back to some of the broader points in the piece. People have said, oh, it's the death of the musical middle class, but we're dealing with the death of *the middle class* right now. The reality now is, we don't have *job* jobs. My parents had jobs where they got up and they went to the same place every day for 30 years, and then they retired with a pension and a watch. And no one in our generation does that. Now, if you want to be an artist, you're an artist, and you drive for Uber, and maybe you rent your spare bedroom on AirBnB, and you also bartend a few nights a week, and you just sort of cobble this living together. And I feel like younger people, because that's always been their reality, are just more comfortable with that than maybe older musicians, who are so used to one path that now that Spotify has come and sort of of upended their path, it's harder for them to deal with.

DM: You know, before streaming, it was still really hard to be a band. But I just feel like today, yeah, this isn't middle class living, what I'm doing, but there is a new space for bands to occupy that wasn't there before.

CH: Let's talk a little bit more about your current economic reality, because you were candid that your Spotify payouts aren't that high.

DM: Yeah.

CH: Do you have a day job? How do you support yourself?

DM: I'm the only one in the band that doesn't have a day job. I do do a bunch of freelance stuff – writing, doing basically any odd jobs – but on the music side of things, you know, we have someone helping us to do our licensing and sync placements. As we mentioned a little bit earlier, just in terms of finding those new revenue streams, those have been really, really helpful for us. We've placed a song in a DirecTV show, an NBC show, and the CW. Those alone are more money than we were making four years ago as a band, and we're also touring. But the other two main members in the band have regular day gigs.

CH: What your band members' other day jobs are?

DM: One of them edits commercials, film-type stuff. He's a digital editor. The other does freelance production for the advertising industry.

CH: For so many generations it was like, "I'm going to quit my day job and become a full-time musician." That was the goal, that was the dream. But in an economy where you don't have a day job, it almost seems easier. I was at South By this year, and one of the big stories down there was this rapper from LA drove to South By, and he had three or four gigs booked, I don't think any of them paid him anything. But he was an Uber driver in LA. He gets to Austin and he finds out his Uber app also works in Austin. So he played gigs, and in between gigs he drove for Uber, and he made $800 driving for Uber in Austin.

I mean, there were people that looked at that and were like "Oh my god, this is horrible," and then there were people that looked at it like "This is great, what else is this guy going to do? He could sit around and watch other bands and eat tacos." I ride in a lot of Ubers, I stay at a lot of AirBnBs. I think both those companies both certainly have plenty of problems, but they also have pretty good products, and, you know, a lot of people I talk to are artists and musicians and actors and actresses, and this is the way that they can fund their creativity and live the life that they want to live and not have to be dependent on "I'm gonna sell a bunch of records, I'm gonna tour and make a bunch of money touring."

DM: If you're realistic that that's not exactly the easiest path, but it's your passion, you can string together so many other opportunities to help fund you along the way that aren't terrible, that aren't going to make you despise – it's not like getting a day job that you're totally frustrated with and you wake up every day dreaming of quitting it. You know, you can string together a lot of ways to help keep funding your creative passion, your creative ambition. I've been doing that – before this band, and I'll still do some solo, kind of singer-songwriter gigs – I haven't had a regular job really since I finished college. And I think if I had had a regular job I wouldn't be talking to you because I probably wouldn't have finished this last record. You gotta make time for your creative work. And that involves not having the burden of a regular everyday routine job.

CH: You're obviously pro-Spotify. But are there ways that Spotify could serve artists better? Maybe it's not more money, though I think everyone would like that. Are there things Spotify could do to be better for artists?

DM: Yeah, I definitely think there are. You know, the payouts are pretty low. But to me, the biggest thing is that I feel like their marketing efforts haven't been the best. I grew up in Indiana. But if I asked a number of people in Indianapolis, or some other bigger towns in Indiana, if they use Spotify, I think a lot of them would even say "I don't know what Spotify is." And so that's one area where, I mean, in terms of expanding their reach, I think it has been hard.

You know, we talked about branding partnerships for bands at the beginning of this interview, I think they're just as important for digital services. For Spotify to increase their paid subscriptions, they're going to have to partner with even bigger companies. I think Starbucks is a great example. I think part of the partnership is they're basically giving every Starbucks employee a six-month free premium subscription. I mean, there's a lot of Starbucks employees, I have no idea how many. But that, I think, is a really, really valuable piece of the puzzle. A lot of people complain that Spotify's payouts aren't that great, and that's true. But that's because three out of four Spotify subscribers aren't paying any money for the service.

CH: Just to be clear, you don't think that Spotify should cut their free tier –

DM: Oh, no. I don't mean to be saying, like, "Everyone's got to pay money," because I think that's actually a terrible idea too. to come back to the piece...one guy on Salon actually implied that I had been paid by Spotify, which is so laughable, I can't even begin to explain. Why Spotify would ever choose the guy who made about $1350 to be their spokesman is beyond my comprehension, but this conversation is really important to have. Lots of people have different opinions on this.

**Kyle Bylin/Tidal**

While the Upward Spiral is generally interview-driven, my co-host Kyle and I will occasionally record a conversation together about a hot topic or new startup. In this episode, we discussed Tidal, the music streaming startup owned by Jay-Z that launched in the spring of 2015.

KYLE BYLIN: Today we talking about Tidal, Jay-Z's new streaming music service.

CORTNEY HARDING: Yeah, this is a very special episode, much like the after-school specials, about the dangers of investing your money in a music startup run by a bunch of artists.

KB: We both watched the press conference today. It really felt to me like an awards show speech was happening, where Alicia Keys was going to present one of the artists there with an award for Best Artist of the Year or Best Dressed. Did you also get that vibe?

CH: Yeah, I got the vibe that no one fully knew what they were doing or what was expected of them, so I noticed that a lot of people missed their cues. When the woman who started it off started introducing people, it took a few beats for some of them to walk on stage. So I think people were just milling around, and then Alicia Keys spoke, it didn't make a lot of sense. She was talking about music and quoting Nietzsche and I was like "Ok, you're making some good points, but you're not explaining the product at all." My great fear was that every artist was going to make that kind of speech and the press conference would have lasted for 10 hours. And then everyone just sort of stood there, and then they signed something, and then that was it.

KB: But Cortney, they signed the declaration of their independence from, presumably, the other streaming companies, from, presumably, the other tech companies in general – maybe even from their own record label management firms, which, of course, is not the case, but it was a very symbolic gesture that we are a lot of powerful artists across a broad range of genres, which I'll hand you to talk about, and here we are on stage at our giant press conference signing this declaration of independence. So, Cortney, tell me who is signing this declaration of independence.

CH: It's interesting, so I'm looking right now, and I just went on Spotify, and Jay-Z's music is all still on there, and interestingly the first result is Jay-Z and Zane Lowe talking to one another – Zane Lowe now famously at Apple, and Jay-Z now famously at Tidal. They might want to take that down. Yeah, the makeup of the crowd – or the makeup of the artists – was, to me, odd, and you could tell that Jay-Z or someone at Roc Nation had a big list, like – "We've gotta get country! So, here we are, Jason Aldean," so he was the token country guy. They had a couple of EDM artists, they had a couple of rock artists, they had a couple of pop artists, it was a nice rainbow coalition of people. That was nice. It wasn't all white people. There were a lot of women, so, yay. It felt very random, and someone tweeted that, "Oh, we actually came up with this as a joke when we were having brunch with Gwyneth and decided to run with it". It was a very weird mishmash of people, and I'm sure their social media managers had a fun day today, and I'm sure their social media managers are the ones who are going to do most of the work.

KB: I think it'd be really interesting to find out, like, who did they approach privately who was like "No, I'm not getting involved with this whole Tidal business." Of course they probably privately reached out to Taylor Swift and she was like "No, I'm not going to do this." But who else did you think they would reach out to?

CH: This is top of mind for me right now because I watched the Scientology documentary last night and I was thinking about when Tom Cruise and Katie Holmes hooked up apparently he had auditions, and approached all of these other young actresses before he came to Katie Holmes, so I'm just imagining Jay-Z and the Illuminati, such as it were. You would have to have a pretty decent chunk of change, and you'd probably have to be kind of tech-savvy, or not tech-savvy – you'd kind of have to be ok with technology. Yeah, Taylor, I'm sure, was obviously like "No." I wonder if Apple is, right now, going to artists and recruiting their little camp of artists. I mean, they've got U2 on board, so there's that. Yeah, I mean, I'm sure they approached a bunch of people who probably took a look at the numbers and went "Eh, not a good fit." Because at the end of the day for these artists, it's mostly about the money, if they've got equity stakes in this, then they have to look at it from a financial perspective.

KB: What is the goal of their artist-owned service? Do they want to grow this and have this great distribution platform that they can promote to their audience and give them some leverage in whatever deals that they're doing? Or are they potentially looking to sell this service to an even higher bidder once they've sprinkled their popular music pixie dust on it and then make a bunch of money that way? I would certainly say they're probably not going to try to go public or anything, that seems out of the question for something any time soon.

CH: People have been talking about Spotify going public for a while now and that still hasn't happened. Yeah, you know, there's probably a little bit of Jay-Z that's probably competitive, and he's like "Oh, Dre got Apple, I can get Google." Which is kind of the only other people that could buy them out?

KB: Yeah, but I mean, Google already bought Songza. They buy all kinds of things. But who else would there be? Maybe Samsung?

CH: Samsung has their own music service.

KB: Yeah, it's Milk, and it's powered by Slacker Radio this time. I think we should talk about – what about the lack of concrete details? So they have the entire world looking at a countdown clock for several hours, then some lady came on stage, introduced Alicia Keys, Alicia Keys introduced a bunch of other people, and then they all signed something, and then there was this vague roundabout about artists owning a streaming service, it showed vague pictures of a streaming service – but it wasn't really high on explaining what Tidal is, why it's valuable, why you should sign up. I felt none of that. In fact, if I closed my eyes, I really thought I was watching the MTV Music Awards and there was some kind of behind-the-scenes trailer that they ran at the end. It didn't seem like an ad to sign this new service up at the moment of peak eyes paying attention to them.

CH: They didn't explain it well at all. But I sort of think they went in with the idea that if you cared enough to watch this livestream you probably already knew what Tidal was already. It would have been nice if they'd said "We're a music streaming service and we have this exclusive content and this and that." I feel like most of the coverage I saw of this press conference was kind of snarky. Everyone was like "Oh, haha, it was all these rich, famous people on stage, with this silly little streaming service." I don't know how many people outside of this bubble actually saw this or cared about it. And I think that's the real problem with Tidal is not that it's a bad service. I don't think it's a great service, but it's certainly not garbage. But it kind of doesn't have an audience.

KB: The current stats found online were 512,000 paying subscribers at the point of acquisition.

CH: I mean, that's not a lot of people.

KB: Let's talk about $19.99/month as a price point. We just read a New York Times story about Apple trying to negotiate down to, say, between $6 and $8 a month, and the record labels are actually saying "Nah, we're not going to let you go down to that price point, we're going to let you stay at $10." Jay-Z's coming out of the gate raising to $20.

CH: I think a lot of people really, really overestimate the market for people who care about audio quality and are willing to pay that much extra for it. The interesting thing to me about the pricing is that usually if there's more competition in the market that drives prices down. So there's a whole bunch of different car companies. And because back in the day you could only buy a Ford, so Ford set the prices. But now I can buy a Ford, or a Honda, or a Kia, or a BMW – and that keeps the prices lower, because there's more competition. But in streaming music, the prices are all essentially the same, essentially, unless you want to go higher. So you can't go lower than $9.99/month. What's interesting about that is then these services, because they can't differentiate on price, they have to differentiate on offering, and there's not that many ways to do that. I mean, Tidal has a video component, which is kind of interesting, it's kind of useful. It's not that hard to open a YouTube window if you want to watch a video, though. So they've got this exclusive video content which is, again, kind of interesting, if I'm really so compelled to watch an Alicia Keys concert from 2 years ago. But there's only so much music out there, and there's only so many times you can get a celebrity to give you a playlist, right? There's only so many ways you can differentiate.

KB: They really did seem to emphasize on this idea of exclusive content, which seems very likely that they have. I would imagine that every one of these artists has a ton of concert video, or B-side tracks that maybe they're just holding on to that could potentially be placed in a service like this, however, I don't think they're holding onto the money-makers, right? Will Tidal, for some of these artists, be a place where they try to debut their primetime music videos before they send them off to the YouTube audience? I think that is a great question to raise, given that the audience there is all behind a paid wall. I'm curious as to whether they go that route.

CH: That's a big risk. If I'm Rihanna, and I have a new single, I'm going to take it to radio. Right? I mean, radio is still king. So it's not like you can set up a deal with Tidal where the only place you can hear this single is on Tidal, because that's just foolish. If you piss off Spotify, fine; if you piss off Z100 that's a world of hurt. The problem is that artificial scarcity makes no sense. So the bigger thing with Tidal is – ok, Rihanna's not going to put her new single on there exclusively, because that's just kind of silly. Yeah, she might put some videos on there, she might put some remixes on there, she might put some B-sides on there – and that's great. Is there anyone out there who's really compelled by this idea of an occasional Rihanna B-side that they're going to pay for something they wouldn't normally pay for?

KB: Here's something that comes to mind when you say that, right, when you are an artist of that size, who is used to paying – people paying attention to whatever it is that you want to do on a given week, you almost have this God complex of whatever I release, everyone's going to be all over, no matter where I release it. And that's, you know, a good mindset to have, but I'm unclear if this really pertains to this very specific, very walled circumstance.

CH: Well, one of the things that I could see being of value in Tidal. SoundCloud and YouTube aside, really, there's no place for artists to just post stuff that they're working on, or just post something that's very timely. If you're an artist in the major label system, there are checks and balances that you have to go through before you can release something and monetize it. So if Tidal can work out some sort of a deal where they've got direct artist deals, and J. Cole wants to write a song about Ferguson, and just wants to put it out immediately and monetize on it? That's something that not a lot of people do, and that's kind of cool. It's a real selling point. It's not like "Oh, I'm going to hear the real official single first," but it's like, I'm an EDM artist, I'm Calvin Harris, and I just made a remix on my computer and I'm just going to throw it up for the world to hear, or throw it up for the Tidal audience to hear – I mean, that's potentially kind of interesting.

KB: Is this going to lead to them retaining their audience? Hey, we got you to sign up for this thing, now stick around for several months while we figure this out.

CH:  signed up for my account and then I put a little note to myself 30 days from now, "cancel Tidal." I'm going to play with it more, but I don't think there's anything compelling enough to switch me from Spotify, even though it's the same price point. I have all my playlists in Spotify, so that's a pain to transfer those, might as well just stay. I can't think of a real reason for anyone to switch. Are younger kids going to care that it's a Jay-Z thing?

KB: I think that's really hard to say, especially at this point in the game.

CH: My guess is that there's not a lot of teenagers out there who are like "Oh my god, this is a Jay-Z thing, I have to do it." If this was – if you got Zayn from One Direction on there, maybe it would be different.

KB: Their new creative director, Zayn from One Direction.

CH: I don't know, older audiences?

KB: The big thing is going to be the lossless audio quality and the audiophiles seeking out a service that will -

CH: But that's such a small market!

KB: It's a very small market at this stage of the game. It could be a profitable one at some point, if they're not trying to do this crazy marketing let's scale to the point of a Spotify, right, in every single market. That's what's expensive, right?

CH: Yeah.

KB: All this scale, all this marketing, all this expansion, all this growth, all these licensing costs – that's what's expensive. If they wanted to keep it a small niche service for audiophiles they could do that.

CH: There's no way they're going to do that. It's run by Jay-Z, I mean – you know, it's got Madonna. Here's the thing. Pono, again, ugh. But at least Pono was like – Neil Young! Rootsy old man stuff! At least Pono, which was a huge flop, made some sense. I mean, if Jack White was running this thing, rather than just part of it, I would give it a little bit more credence, but – this has Nicki Minaj on board. I will say this, most people who are audiophiles are probably dudes and they're probably older. I apologize if there's any young women who are audiophiles, I'm just – broad stripes here. And they're not going to care. Even if the quality is incredible, it's such a small market. And because they set themselves up as having this huge catalog and these huge names, it's going to be impossible.

KB: Well, and especially if the limit of their involvement is "Hi, I'm Nicki Minaj, an owner of Tidal. We're an artist owned service with exclusive content. Thank you so much for listening to my brand new playlists of artists I like with a few B-sides of mine." You can just hear the promo of her talking about what she did.

CH: Yeah, I'll be totally honest. Today I listened to Beyonce's spring playlist, because I love Beyonce, and I know Beyonce didn't put that together, her assistant put it together, or her assistant's assistant put it together. It's the exact same thing as when Nicki Minaj has a deal with Pepsi, or Coke, or whomever she has a deal with. They give her a script, and she reads the script, she gets a check, and she goes and does something else. For all these artists, this is basically just another product endorsement deal.

KB: At this stage in the game, I don't think a lot of people understand that Pandora isn't just an app on my phone, it's a real place in Oakland, California, that has hundreds of employees who are making this thing run. So, it's almost even too meta to say, "Nicki Minaj isn't really involved, it's actually her social media coordinator putting together her playlists and maybe recording a quick blurb from Nicki and then it's done, put it on the site."

CH: Yeah. I mean, Alicia Keys is involved in this in the same way that she was the creative director of Blackberry.

KB: Boom.

CH: Justin Timberlake – well, he's not involved in this, but he's the creative director of Budweiser, or something, right? I feel like Jay-Z was the creative director of something for a while. Someone said "Jay-Z is rich and bored." He's not doing the Nets any more, he just sits around on a pile of money and he's like "Eh, I'll buy a streaming service, that sounds fun. Dre's not the only one who gets this." I'm sure a lot of these artists have good intentions, I'm sure some of them do care about music, I'm not saying they're all full of it – but yeah, this is a product endorsement deal for them, and their involvement is going to be very limited. Tidal, and the parent company, they've got bunch of Nordic engineers who are probably making the thing run day to day in an office in Stockholm, or Oslo, or wherever. There's plenty of people at Roc Nation, I'm sure, who are working on this. There's a whole bunch of non-glamorous people behind all of this making it actually run.

KB: I was reading something the other day that talked about "Oh, Trent Reznor is now overseeing the product development for iTunes Radio and Beats, whatever revamp he's more involved in." With all due respect, I think Trent Reznor is incredibly smart, I bet he brings a lot to the table and has a very nuanced perspective about how to make this better. But he's not a technical cofounder or necessarily a product visionary per se. Well, that's probably what he is, is the product visionary, which is the kind of guy that's like "There's not enough soul in the music player, Cortney, I need more soul in here."

CH: Do you need more soul, Trent, or do you need *my* soul, so you can eat it? That was Trent Reznor 20 years ago.

KB: Where's the art? Where's the art in music, Cortney? You can just really hear these esoteric, high-level statements being made, where some real person is like "Ok, I've gotta develop some code for this, how do you want it to work? And will the thing that you want it to work like actually appeal to people and make sense?" Because then that's the other question, does the thing we're building make any sense?

CH: Trent Reznor's not a product manager, right? He doesn't go sit in an office in Cupertino every day. There's a staff that does that., Jay-Z is not the guy who's, like, designing the UX. Part of me just really questions how engaged people are with a lot of these artists that were up on stage today. Like, how many people are actually going to be interested in this because of somebody tweeting about it? Honestly, Kanye should have brought Kim Kardashian. That probably would have gotten a much bigger response.

KB: I think you're touching on the most important question that's been at the center of the discussion for a while, which is – if social media isn't that great at selling records, how will it sell a subscription media service?

CH: I think it was Bret Michaels, or it was someone who was like an aging '80s rocker, who put out an album, and he said "I have 100,000 likes on Facebook, and my album sold 1,000 copies." The thing with social media is that it's such a low-impact investment. I follow hundreds of people on Twitter, but I don't particularly care that much, or convert because of them. People I actually know and like and follow on socials, I'm much more likely to engage with. The bands I follow on Twitter, mostly because I want to know what their tour dates are, or I'm like "Oh, you've got a new single out, awesome, I'll check it out at some point." So yeah, the idea that Madonna can sell me on a streaming service? Even Beyonce can't sell me on a streaming service at that point. I'm like, "Eh."

KB: Maybe they'll relaunch the service as "All the Single Ladies."

CH: Yes. Actually, I have to say – if Beyonce had launched it it probably would have gotten a better response.

KB: But Beyonce would have launched it without telling anyone, and there would have been no press conference, it would have been like "I just launched a streaming service, boom, it's out there. Go check out my latest art videos on there."

CH: For me that would have been way more exciting, personally. The thing with Tidal, honestly, is that it feels unnecessary. It's a totally decent service, it just feels, in the crowded market, totally unnecessary. The only thing that it has selling it are a bunch of celebrities on a stage. You know, the whole artist friendliness thing. I'm like "Yeah, you have a bunch of famous artists who have equity" – but that doesn't trickle down. I mean, and I say this really not liking this guy – I would have really liked to see David Lowery on that stage. Right? Or Dean Wareham, or any of these people who are really anti-streaming because they're pro-artist. If those people are getting compensated in a way that I think is fair, I'm like "Ok, this is really a pro-artist service." Right now, I mean – my guess, and I don't know, but my guess is all the other deals were just carryover deals from whatever deal that Tidal had with the other artists before.

KB: I think you just raised a really important point, which is an issue I'm pretty sure I saw someone tweet, which is – when is a reporter going to ask Jay-Z, "So, what is the per-stream rate? How does it stack up against these other services? Is it artist-friendly because it's artist-owned? Or are you actually going to be paying out more of your revenues to these artists? Or is it just the fact that once this thing gets acquired, if it does, all the money goes to those big-name artists on stage?"

CH: Well, I mean, Jay-Z has been saying, again, "Oh, we're going to pay better, we're going to be more transparent, I'm all about transparency" – and that's admirable, but he has not said "Our per-stream rate is going to be x." You know, I think it's – again, it might be the same as Spotify, where you can't determine the per-stream rate because there are just so many other confounding factors that go into that. It's not like Pandora, where there's a set rate. So, I don't know. I think on balance, it's good for artists, because the more outlets there are, even if they're making pennies per whatever from each outlet, that still adds up. I think artist-friendly is going to be a hard term to define in this context.

KB: Well, and it's going to sort of be harder to define because every single streaming music company has made inroads on this in the last two years, right? Pandora has an entire artist dashboard with data. They're allowing these interstitial audio ads to be placed inside stations, where it says "Hi, I'm Nicki Minaj, go buy my new album." And Spotify has been doing their own data dashboard for a while, as well as other artist initiatives that I haven't kept up on. I think Deezer for artists exists. And this has been two, three years in the making of streaming music services getting very smart about their PR in an age where they're being criticized for these paltry royalty payments.

So I feel like at this point it'll have to be more than lip service of "We're artist-friendly," where you have a lot of other really big companies saying "You know, you might not think that we're artist-friendly, but, look, we're putting real resources behind making this service more valuable to you, providing data for you, helping you make decisions with your fanbase and your marketing."

CH: At the end of the day, Tidal doesn't have ads, so they don't have the freemium revenue stream with ads, you know – it's going to be hard for them to pay anything close to Spotify, not because they're trying to rip off artists, but because they're going to have a real hard time growing an audience. I think it's going to be really tough for them to get big.

KB: And this is also the most important point, right, is that a lot of really smart people have been trying to crack this particular nut for a really long time, and as big as they are, despite all of those smart people, all of that venture capital money, and all of that marketing, quite frankly, Tidal coming in the market and now saying "We're going to leverage celebrities and social media to get people on board for this service" – that's great, Apple can do that too. No one is doing anything at this stage in the game that the other person can't go "All right, Jay-Z, we'll do that too."

CH: Yeah. I see your Jay-Z and raise you a Dr. Dre, or your Jay-Z and raise you an Eminem, or – my fear is it's going to turn into this arms race of celebrity endorsements, and it's going to turn into an arms race of exclusivity.

KB: And what happens when you do that? The world starts looking a lot like Netflix and Hulu.

CH: Right. Which is two players. You know, essentially. And Netflix and Hulu have different – there's crossover but they're different enough products. I mean, yeah. There's going to be one or two companies standing in the end. Maybe there are ways that they sort of differentiate themselves in ways that more companies can coexist and have an audience, but – yeah. You know, there's no serious Netflix competitor.

KB: An important thing to say, though, is that this isn't apples to apples, either.

CH: Right.

KB: When you're turning on Netflix, you're turning on television, which means you're lounging on your couch, and you're checking out, and you're watching whatever is there. Your bar can be pretty low sometimes. When you're going to listen to music, you're not just like "Oh, let me go through the little turnstile of the 20 albums on Tidal this month and listen to those 20 albums," you kind of might be specific at times, and if you can't play the thing you want, you'll just go somewhere you can.

CH: Right. And you get that with Netflix and Hulu as well. I have Netflix, and I have Amazon Prime streaming, and then I have Popcorn Time. And I'm like "Well, if I can find it on Netflix, I guess I'll go find it on Popcorn Time." I feel a little bit bad about that, but not that bad, because if they really wanted me to pay for it, they'd put it on Netflix. I don't think you'll get a lot of people who are like "I'm going to sign up for Tidal and then I'll have 2 streaming services!"

Here's the thing. There's no urgency with listening to music. I can only think of 1 or 2 bands who I'd *really* make the effort to listen to an album as soon as it came out. Everyone else? I can wait a week. It doesn't matter that much. There's no way to spoil a record, right? I was talking to someone about TV – I have to watch Mad Men when it airs, because otherwise it'll get spoiled for me. But if someone says, like, "Oh, the Kendrick Lamar album's really good, and he samples lots of different stuff, and he raps about social issues," that doesn't spoil it for me. That makes me want to listen to it more. So it's not a big deal if I wait a week or more to listen to the Kendrick record. I'll get to it. So there's less of a sense of urgency. So then doubling down on exclusives – people will just wait it out. Unless you're talking about a really young audience, people will just wait. They're like "Eh, I'll hear it when I hear it, I'll just listen to something else."

KB: Several years ago, Anthony at Hype Machine did an essay where he described this effect called the Minesweeper Effect, which is this idea that if you go into a streaming music service and you top in the top 5 artists that come to mind, if they're not there, you blow up, it's Minesweeper, and they just go do something else. It's not like they restart the process of the other 5 artists that they know and then continue listening to the service. I would say it's more likely that they're like "Oh, wow, Frightened Rabbit and New Found Glory aren't on Tidal, ok, well, I don't really want to listen to other things, that's actually what I want to listen to right now." I believe what you said, that some people are going to be willing to sacrifice and say "Oh, well, the new Kendrick Lamar album isn't there right now, so let me just check out this track by Jay-Z," but I think it's the duality, right?

On the one hand you have the people who just want to hit the button, they want the music to play, and they'd like to be entertained while they do something else. The minute they want to lean in and hear the new Taylor Swift song and find out it's not there, they probably will be a little bit miffed, and then you have the people for whom dictate to the service what they want to hear at different times, and if that specific music isn't going to be there, why would they continue paying for the service? And that, by the way, describes the music fanatic, someone who specifically knows what they want to listen to at any given time in the day and seeks it out. That's the definition of lean forward. So if you can't lean forward into Tidal and listen to the music that you want, I think that's going to be a problem for them with that high-end audience.

CH: Yeah, that's going to be a huge problem. I don't think Tidal actually has a problem with not having enough content. Their content seems pretty complete. At any given time there's 5 or 6 things I want to listen to. So if Kendrick Lamar isn't available to me, the catalog is complete enough where there's a bunch of other stuff I can listen to and then I'll wait a week and listen to the Kendrick album then. Yeah, if I was going to a service where they didn't have *anything* I wanted, that would be very bad. I will say this for Tidal, they have a pretty cool international catalog. They had a great Ethiopian jazz playlist that I really liked. The Norwegian jazz playlist was interesting, kind of trippy. So I like that, the sort of deeper curation, for sure.

I think just getting into this exclusives arms race helps no one, except maybe labels. But even then – I think you leave so much money on the table when you make your product artificially scarce. I don't know when the whole exclusivity war started, I think it was post-Napster and it was to cater to the Wal-Marts and the Targets of the world, but whoever started it really sucks, and now it's turned into this really ridiculous – again, Tidal's offering the exclusive of an Alicia Keys concert from 2 years ago. I guess people want to watch that? I guess? I don't know. That's not a very good exclusive.

KB: I have not logged in to Tidal myself. To answer your point, of *course* I don't think an exclusive Alicia Keys concert from 2 years ago is going to be content that keeps people in the door and engaged with the service. If anything, that was a poor example of what this was supposed to be capable of and the kinds of promises that were made on that stage today.

CH: I'm scrolling through the main page. So it's Alicia Keys from 3 years ago, Daft Punk's feature-length film, an old White Stripes concert, and then a bunch of playlists. Coldplay's playlist, which is really Coldplay's assistant's playlist. Again, Arcade Fire made a playlist, like, all right. And then you have a bunch of stuff that's probably on Spotify. You have Rival Sons, you have this kind of cool jazz playlist. Tobias Jesso, Jr. Kendrick

Lamar! This is all stuff you can get everywhere else. Again, it's good quality stuff – they have a really good Emmylou Harris playlist that I liked – but this is not the only place you can hear Beyonce's new song ever. It's like, here's an Alicia Keys concert from 2012. It's not compelling content at this point, especially for launch day. I'd think for launch day they'd have Beyonce's Meerkat stream or something.

KB: That is the perfect tech example to make. Exclusive Meerkat content from your favorite artists on Tidal.

CH: I'm looking at it and it's not bad, it's just not – given that press conference, and I know that these things are pretty much worthless – I was really expecting more.

KB: Exactly. I was expecting a lot more too, being so attuned to how Apple does their press conferences, I expected so much more focus on their product, I expected to be blown away by what they came together to do, and I was expecting a really clear and concise story, which I feel like we got none of today.

CH: Yeah.

KB: Just a lot of big names on a stage talking esoterically about music and what it meant to them, and signing some document – *some document!* – that we're just jokingly referring to as the declaration of their independence. Then they ran a promo reel for the service of them talking about the thing that they were going to do. Then they cut the stream. It's like, ok, we did it, bye.

CH: This was a whole lot of nothing. And I feel like we've seen more and more of that recently. There's so many artists now, oh, they're hyping up, "Oh, I have a new thing coming out, here's my countdown clock," and then it's like "Oh, here's my new perfume!" or "Hey, it's a 30-second clip of my new single!" And it's like – all that buildup for *that*? And this was a triumph of marketing over technology, is really what it boils down to. In terms of marketing, this was an A+ home run. Everyone I knew on Twitter was tweeting about this. Everyone I knew was watching this livestream and cracking wise and it's totally won Twitter today. But it's won Twitter *today*. Something else is going to win Twitter tomorrow. And the product – I feel like a) the product – I feel like very few people know what the product is, and b) the product is not special. And, you know, this is totally hype over actual product. I mean, maybe the product will get better? Maybe they'll add some really cool stuff, maybe they'll do some really cool stuff, but honestly? Eh. I don't know. I think this was a whole lot of hot air.

## Kyle Bylin/YouTube

While people love to chat about Spotify, Apple Music, and other streaming services, the fact is that YouTube eats all their lunches when it comes to being a destination for music. Not only is YouTube free and complete, it's become a hub for teens and early twenty-somethings, who consume more content on there than they do on traditional TV. Kyle and I chatted about YouTube and music videos, and how streaming services can compete.

KB: Cortney, you wrote a piece on Medium about how YouTube, which plays music videos, is actually competing for the attention of these other streaming music services because it also provides on-demand music for free, which you don't have to do anything for,, you just have to watch an ad. Why do you think it was time to bring that into the discussion?

CH: I felt that Tidal just launched, everyone's excited for what Apple's going to do with Beats whenever they're going to launch it, and – you know, Spotify is still raising money, Spotify's still a big product, and there's all these other – Deezer, rdio, and secondary competitors, and people tend to get kind of myopic about what defines a streaming service. But Ethan Kaplan said it best on Twitter, and this is how I opened the piece, it was like: "Millions of kids watched the Tidal announcement, sort of shrugged and went back to YouTube." And if you look at where younger people, who, as we know, are a big chunk of the music audience, are consuming media – it's on YouTube. The problem is – Spotify and Deezer and Tidal and all these other companies are competing with each other for a very small segment of the market, but YouTube is eating their lunch. Part of it is that everything is on YouTube.

I'll give you an example. Last night was the South African Music Awards, which I know not a lot of people in the US care about, obviously, but I have a friend who's down there, she's a music person down there, and she happened to be live tweeting it. So I was killing time Sunday night, and I was like "These are some cool sounding bands, let me check these guys out." So I was on Spotify, and there was nothing on there for most of those bands. And these are not – they're independent bands, some of them, but they're big enough to win music awards in a decent sized music market. They're not a little bar band. None of them are on Spotify. And I'm like "Ok, go to YouTube." They're all on YouTube. Tons of videos, tons of content. And I thought, after about two or three failures on Spotify, "The heck with that," and just watched everything on YouTube. And all the live stuff is on there. All the clips are on there. All the lyric videos are on there. Anything that Tidal promotes as exclusive is on there within 20 minutes. People just want stuff when they want it. They don't want to have to jump through all these hoops, which is what we've been seeing for a long time now with media consumption. And I just feel like Spotify and Tidal and all those guys can kind of scrap it out, but at the end of the day I think most people just go to YouTube.

KB: What we forget is that when someone has a song that they want to hear, their first instinct, their first gut reaction is "I'm going to go look that up on YouTube." 9 times out of 10 if not 10 out of 10, it's going to be on YouTube somewhere, available to stream. I remember a music industry commentator a few years ago said "It's like the Minesweeper effect. If you go into a streaming music service and you start hitting dials and something's not there, you – Minesweeper. You hit a mine and it blows up the game." And when fans do that when they encounter a music streaming service, they can only Minesweeper a few times before they get frustrated and go "Ugh, they don't have the things that I want to listen to, why am I going to pay for it." Maybe that's giving too much status to this idea that if fans can't find something they'll go somewhere else. Maybe if they can't find what they're looking for they'll just stream something else entirely; they don't care whether Jay-Z's "Glory Song" is on Spotify or Tidal. If it's not there, it's just not there. They lose that window of attention that Jay-Z was given at that time.

CH: I think there's a good argument to be said for "Look, a lot of these services – if you can't find something, you can go somewhere else, or you go something else on that service." I think part of the problem is, you know, if I'm looking for something on Spotify all I get is a blank. So last night I typed in the name of an artist on Spotify and I just "We don't have that." Rather than "You're looking for that South African R&B singer. We don't have her, but we have four other artists who sound similar to her." Or something. Part of it is that they throw up their own roadblocks sometimes. I think it's one thing if a streaming service says "Ok, we don't have this content, but we have similar content." The problem is they don't redirect you in any way. All you get is this dead end where it's like "We don't have this." You're like "Ok, what do I do with that."

KB: There's a setting on Spotify that allows you to hide content that isn't available in the service, so if you were going to go look for Taylor Swift's 1989, and you have that checked, it just won't show up in her Artist Results page. Whereas if you do have it checked to see that hidden content, it'll just show up but you can't do anything with it. So who knows, maybe Spotify does have those artists listed in the service, but you've chosen to hide the content, therefore it doesn't show up at all.

CH: Right, but I'm not even talking about this artist doesn't show up vs. they do show up but I can't play it, I'm talking about not – so, ok, fine, I hit an end, I hit a wall because they don't have it, but they don't send me anywhere else. So if I'm looking for Taylor Swift, it's not going to say "Try some LeAnn Rimes," or any given artist, it's just going to say "Sorry, we don't have that." So that was really more what I was getting to – you have to be really self-directed. And after a while, again, of brick wall after brick wall after brick wall, I'm like "Eh, I'll just go to YouTube, because they're gonna have something."

KB: And whatever you find, there's always the rabbit hole that you can go down with the recommended music videos that tend to be pretty on point about other things you might be interested in, and then you have the autoplay factor of once you've finished watching something, it often cues up something right behind that that you get into and start watching.

CH: Yep, exactly. I went into a couple rabbit holes last night and, again, discovered some more cool new stuff. The problem with YouTube is that the product is not very good. The content is great, the – everything getting cued up and played is great – but a lot of the – again, there was a lot of problems with YouTube, but I think the good generally outweighs the bad. Especially when you're like "YouTube is free, or YouTube is the cost of your 30 seconds to pay attention to an ad," which it's really easy to just mute. That's what I do. That's my cheat. Versus Spotify, where – again, you keep hitting these brick walls, eventually – and again, I don't hit enough brick walls on Spotify to cancel my subscription, but I'm a power user. If you're not a power user, you sign up, you hit a bunch of brick walls, and then you cancel your account.

KB: So what you're talking about there is the promise of YouTube Music Key, though. What they've done is streamlined the service. They've hidden some of the content that may not be as relevant as the stuff that you're looking for. They've grouped the specific content from a specific artist under their page as opposed to everything in the river, and my understanding is that they've made it easier to create playlists and potentially even engage in YouTube as a station-like experience, or as a personalized station experience. What they seem to be trying to do is now offer this premium version of YouTube that is going to take out a lot of this nascent annoying time-consuming browsing and make it into a streamlined experience that you're going to have to pay $9.99/month to access. The question is whether or not people are willing to pay $9.99/month to access that more streamlined version. I don't know. What do you think?

CH: I think if they ever get it out of beta then we'll have an answer. YouTube doesn't seem to care that much. They built Music Key, they sort of threw it out there, they were like 'Eh, let's launch it,' and that was what – November? And it's the end of April? And it's still in Beta? This is Google, people. If they wanted to build something really good, they could have built something good. These people are building a car that drives itself – they could have built a music streaming platform off YouTube. So, you know, clearly something is happening. It's almost never part of their advertisements, right? They're much more invested in their own content – which is fine, but, you know, it is 40% of their traffic. That's the thing. The rate that artists get paid per stream off of YouTube is far lower than Spotify, and what's very funny – everyone loves to hate Spotify, but no one loves to hate YouTube, unless it's Prince. There's a lot of artists that are not complaining about YouTube. They're complaining about Spotify. Just putting it out there – Spotify pays you more. So, yeah, I think that – YouTube could build something really great. They're not choosing to, for, I'm sure, any number of internal reasons. But if YouTube put out a really great product, that could be bad for a lot of other companies.

KB: So you touched on a lot of things there. I think the most important thing to touch on is – what is a music video? Who is it for? And where does it fit inside the record label toolkit of artist promotion? What I mean by that is – when music video started out, it was very clear that this was a promotional video sent to television to raise awareness for the artist and to sell albums. These days, it's becoming less clear what the goal of a music video is. Of course it's there to raise attention for the artist, to sell the single, to potentially go viral and bring in a whole wider fan base than the artist would have been previously capable of, but people are consuming music videos on demand as if they were the product. They're just streaming them multiple times in a row and getting their fix from the music video and not necessarily needing to pay the $0.99 to be able to take it with them on their phone. So I think we're entering a point where record labels have to ask themselves – have we really differentiated the difference between an on-demand music video and an on-demand song stream? Obviously the products are a world of difference from each other, but to the consumer, who just wants to play a song, they're getting directly what they want from YouTube and they're not really paying anything. Obviously they're paying in their attention – they're seeing the ad, they're seeing who sponsored the ad, and they're potentially seeing all kinds of brands and product placement inside that music video, but they as the consumer aren't directly exchanging money with YouTube for that offering or contributing money to artists at all.

CH: Yeah, I think that's exactly right. You know, there's a little bit of analogy to MTV, right? You had to pay for MTV in the sense that you had to pay for cable, but you are paying for YouTube in the sense that you have to pay for the internet connection, right? So yeah, it's kind of the same. The thing is with MTV – they control the programming. With YouTube, you essentially control the programming. So, you know, part of it goes back to a lot of the precedents that were set many years ago, where – in the US, and I know that this is not the case internationally – but in the US, artists don't get paid for radio play. That's one of the funny things about people being angry about Pandora is – yeah, you got zero from being on the radio. You get not much from being on Pandora, but being on terrestrial radio in the US, you got nothing. And it's the same with MTV, right? MTV didn't pay for those videos, artists didn't get paid for those videos. So, you know, labels sort of set this precedent back, I guess, in the '50s, and then again in the '80s, where – now it's very easy for someone like YouTube to say "Oh, it's just like MTV. It's just promotion. So, you know, give us this video." I do think that – you know, it's funny, because I think music video budgets have gone way down, because it's so much cheaper to make a cool music video, and I think their importance has actually kind of skyrocketed. Especially for emerging artists or quirkier artists – Psy is sort of the famous one – but no way in hell Psy would have gotten big pre-YouTube. There's no way that video would have been on MTV, except for maybe as a joke. And Psy legitimately had a really huge hit because of a really cool video. And I feel like people – it's much easier to pass videos around. They're very shareable. So I feel like for the labels – it should be where they're spending time, because that's the dominant way I think people are viewing music content. And I think for labels it's also easy to just throw everything up and make a lyric video. I see a lot of albums come out where it's just like, one or two official videos and then ten lyric videos come out and people are just like "Oh, that's just so I can listen to it."

KB: One important thing to add [to] what you were saying before is that songwriters do make money when their music is played on the radio. Historically, bands have cut themselves as equal part songwriter on a specific work, therefore they've all fairly contributed when their music is played on radio. They didn't want to create a conflict where Dave Grohl, for example, gets all of the money from radio and all of the other band members are left empty-handed.

CH: Right, that's true. I should have been more specific when I talked about that.

KB: The other thing I would add to what you're saying is – lyric videos have this capacity to be addictive in their own right, because for a lot of people lyrics are what they care about. They want to know the words, they want to sing along with them. And when they're done right, lyric videos are fairly compelling. They're not free to make, but they are cheaper than renting a location, hiring a bunch of actors and people on the set to film it, among the myriad of other things that go into producing a video and video content. What's interesting about videos today is that they're now evolving video content to an immersive experience. Increasingly you're having videos that are offered as either a 360 degree angle, which recently came out, wherein if you open the video in a Chrome browser, you yourself can rotate the viewpoint of the camera to see the entirety of what's happening in the music video. So if in front of you in the video the lead singer is singing and dancing around, you can scroll backwards and see where the band is performing on a specific track and also see a certain number of easter eggs, if you will, that are packed into the video for that reason. There's also been live concerts with multiple angles where you can focus in on the woman playing the song, you can scroll back and see the camera panning throughout the rest of the set, and you can even take a look at the other guitarist. It's really neat because it unfolds in real time; you get to personalize this experience and take different viewpoints on it. The question I have with multi-angle or 360 degree videos as they exist today is whether that quote-unquote immersive experience, that personalization, is a novelty that wears off over time, and whether or not that's something that fans want.

CH: Well, I just remember the Arcade Fire video that came out four or five years now, so it was a while ago, where you could plug in your address, or the address of your childhood home, and it would take you around your neighborhood. It was like a Google Maps hack. And that was really cool, and I remember liking that a lot and playing with that a lot. Yeah, I mean, look. I think once everyone does a cool immersive video that'll be over, but I also think, you know, again, I was part of a music video performance with Oculus Rift, and that was cool. And again, five years from now, I could be like "Another Oculus Rift music video, who cares," but right now that's really interesting. And I feel like there's – there's a lot of cool stuff that artists are doing and can do, and bring in totally different talent sets. You know, like bring in different hackers, and bring in different programmers, and bring in different platforms – there's a lot of cool stuff artists can do with music videos. And, again, you know, it doesn't cost, comparatively, that much. I watched the last season of Empire, and while it's a fun show, it's really dated, and part of what's really dated is that there's an argument over "We need a $3 million music video budget," and you've got the kid in a hot tub with a bunch of women, and you've got him on a jet ski, and you've got him making it rain at the strip club, and all these outdated tropes. And I was just like "Yeah, that's not how it is any more." I feel like if you put out a music video like that, without the winking acknowledgement that it's a joke, people would just sort of shrug. And I feel like the next step is "Let's build something really clever and really cool that people can get into," because, again, it goes back to the idea that people don't want to be passive consumers any more. They want experiences. Again – I've said this before – but people won't pay $10 a month to stream music, but they'll pay $400 to go to Coachella – or *thousands* to go to Coachella. I mean, people would – I'd probably get bored if it was like "Oh, another music video." But if I can plug in my address, or, you know, flip the channels, like – that's pretty compelling. So, yeah, there's a lot that can be done with music videos on the higher end. And on the lower end – you're right, lyric videos probably cost – I'm sure an intern could make a lyric video at this point. Some of them sure look like an intern made them. But people don't care.

KB: You're burying the lede there. Tell us what it was like to experience a music video inside Oculus Rift.

CH: So this wasn't exactly a music video. This was a performance by an artist named Ema – E-M-A, who's excellent and you should listen to her. She did an art exhibition where she had worked with a designer, they programmed a bunch of different environments, and then she played live – and she played all these different songs for hours, all these different song cycles, and people basically – it was a circular room – you stood in line, and you watched her play while you were standing in line, and you sat behind her on stage with your Oculus Rift on for two minutes, and you got to see these different environments through your Oculus Rift and interact and look around and see all the crazy stuff that she and this designer had made, and it was incredible. It was really, really, really cool. That obviously something that had to be staged; it was an art show, but I imagine as more and more people start to get these glasses, they could be – again, you could work with these designers and it could become more and more experiential. So you put on your Oculus Rift and you queue up a video, and it's a Choose Your Own Adventure video, which I think is incredible, and I think it's a tremendously cool immersive experience to have, much cooler than sitting and staring at a screen.

KB: So recently, with the debut of Taylor Swift's video for "Blank Space," she recently released an app that allows you to go inside the music video itself and experience it almost like you were there. It isn't quite as in-depth as an Oculus Rift experience would be, but you're holding your smartphone screen a few feet from your eyes, and whether you tilt it down, up or spin around in your chair, you see all the aspects of this lively mansion as Taylor Swift is swooning in front of this guy. And while you can't walk around as if you were inside the music video, if you touch any of the doors, it carries you to the next room, and you can look around at things as if you were there. You can sit and stare down at the table, you can glance around at the walls, and imaginably, as time goes on, as it becomes more of an Oculus Rift-like experience, you will be able to walk around inside the music video itself and will be able to interact with the environment in some way, and arguably this idea of native advertising could come to mean something entirely different inside of this virtual world, wherein items on a table or in a virtual closet are actual brand – product placements that you are interacting with and experiencing in real time inside of that music video.

CH: And that's the the Kim Kardashian iPhone app – that was huge, and that was such a profitable app, because you could buy all these in-app purchases. People talk about how do musicians monetize – that's a great idea. Create an immersive in-app environment – and Taylor Swift is a perfect case study for this, right – you're looking at the table while Taylor is swooning off in the other room with whomever she's dating, so it's like "Oh, Taylor's blouse? Do I want Taylor's blouse? Sure, I'll buy that." And Taylor gets a cut. Clearly that's not something everyone can do, but for artists like a Taylor or a Beyonce, I'd spend my life savings on that app. And even if you're not a Taylor Swift or a Beyonce, again, putting those branded experiences inside the app – "Oh, hey, this table is made by Crate & Barrel. Interesting. I can go into the kitchen and drink a Pepsi." There's so much more that can be done there, and this is just the tip of the iceberg.

KB: Something that's worth noting is that creative immersive experiences, creating addictive games, isn't necessarily a cut & paste experience. You do need to hire experts in this to really put forth a compelling product, and that product could fail on its face and still cost potentially tens, if not hundreds of thousands of dollars, because, let's be honest, developers aren't free these days. They know what they're worth and they're building all kinds of things. So we are talking about the 1% of artists who could create a compelling experience but may not be able to replicate what Kim Kardashian has done with her app and the number of conversions she has been able to do inside of that game experience.

CH: Ok, so, fine. If you're talking about a Kim Kardashian-style thing, you're right, that's for Taylor and Beyonce and Katy Perry. But don't forget here that the brands are getting a cut of this stuff, and that there are a lot of brands here with a lot of money who are willing to work with bands that aren't the 1% of artists. So baby bands certainly won't be able to do this, and that is what it is, but if you're a mid-level band, if you're a cool rock band, you know, cool indie-ish rock band, there's probably a beer sponsor that would probably love to do a cool immersive video where you're, like, out at a bar with Pabst Blue Ribbon signs everywhere. That's something a beer company would put some money towards. And once they've built that framework they can probably replicate it with different bands. So, yeah, the real high-level sort of Kardashian stuff is going to be reserved, but even the sort of mid-level bands with brand partners could potentially build really interesting things.

KB: Well, and the landscape of that has changed, too, because, you know, these native advertising companies that are allowing artists to put brand sponsoring inside of their music videos after they've already been recorded. So if you sign up a deal with Grand Marnier, rum or Bud Light, you can figure out how to place those products inside your music video after it's already happened. So if Bud Light is doing a campaign promoting a specific brand, whether it's Bud Light Premium or something else they've concocted, you can go to Bud Light and say "Hi, I'm Jason deRulo, I have this many music video views every single month. We have ways to place your product inside all of my music videos in a way that aligns with your campaign." It's no longer a music video team approaching a brand and trying to get products placed in the video before it happens, it's a combination of record labels and brands working together to run campaigns for a native advertising inside music videos long after they've been recorded.

CH: Well, the other thing is, too, and I don't know this, so I could be wrong, but I would guess that Mirriad, which is the company that does this native in-video advertising, they make it possible to geo-target your ads, so, I don't know, say you're Jason deRulo, and you want to grow in the Middle East. Obviously you're not going to have alcohol sponsors in the Middle East, but you might have a food sponsor or a clothing sponsor or any number of any sponsors. So if you could geo-target and say you're going to do a deal with, say, Budweiser in the US, and Pepsi in the Middle East, and another local brand in Southeast Asia – I mean, that could get pretty big pretty fast and open up a lot of other markets very quickly. So, you know, I don't know if that's do-able, but if it is, that's pretty awesome, and it's pretty awesome if you're trying to break artists from other countries, because, again, if you have an artist from a different territory, even if they've shot a video with all non-American brands, it's pretty easy to swap those out and be like "Oh, she's got Bud Light in her video," instead of a South Korean beer or something.

KB: With technology, eventually someone will figure it out, it just depends on whether they figure it out at a time where they can scale and make money and make a lot of these promises happen. I'd have to imagine with campaigns of this potential that there would be significantly more interesting data tied to the consumers that are seeing the ads and their rate of then interacting with those products in the market. I know that there's research that, I believe, came from Nielsen Entertainment that said when brands and products are placed in a music video, they get an 8% lift in awareness and intent to purchase from people who are exposed to them in the music videos, so there's real data saying that people are seeing these ads, they are purchasing these products, and artists are good marketers for those brands.

CH: That's a huge part of it, is when you look at it – when you look at what YouTube pays artists, that's not an entire representation. So yeah, YouTube pays artists x per stream, or x per video view, or whatever, but it's also giving artists a platform to monetize their content in different ways. So, you know, again, if I am Taylor Swift, that's kind of an obvious case, everything in my video is probably monetized, but even if I'm a cool indie band from Brooklyn, I go to Converse and I say "Ok, I'll wear your shoes in the video, give me a couple grand. Hey, I'll wear your leather jackets in the video. I'll drink your beer in the video." And eventually it just becomes background. Like, I know full well that there are many, many paid placements in many of the TV shows and movies that I watch, and I just started noticing it that much. Unless it's very, very noticeable where someone, like, takes a Pepsi out of the fridge and holds it up to the camera and smiles, you know, then it's kind of cheesy, but – I could go through a lot of the TV shows I watch and go "Oh, they have this type of computer, they have this type of product, or they're all driving Chevys," and you kind of subliminally notice it, but it doesn't hit you over the head. And so I feel like with music videos it'll become the same thing, where there's a lot of product placement but it all just is sliding by in the background, and you're subliminally picking it up, but you're not like "Oh, so-and-so sponsored this video? That's lame."

KB: Well, it's going to be clear who sponsored it if someone is using a Microsoft surface instead of an Apple iPad.

CH: Well, that's true.

KB: So you do have these moments where it's abundantly clear that a new company is coming out with a product and that they've sponsored it to be in that video. Pretty soon we're going to see a lot of rappers wearing Apple Watches, and I feel like that's not going to be on accident. They're going to make sure that those relationships, that luxury brand, is being promoted by people that kind of have the affluence and money to flaunt an Apple Watch as something that everyone else in the world will want.

CH: Yeah. And whoever competes with Apple Watches – I'm sure someone is going to come out with a competitor and they're going to find a couple rappers, and it's like "Ooh, you've got a Samsung watch on." That's the new rap beef, is who's paying for your watch. But again – it's a revenue stream that artists and labels can get a crack at. I'm sure that it happened back in the days of MTV, but MTV had a much higher gate to clear, to get on MTV, right? So anyone – again, going back to Psu, Psy put up the video – and I know Psy didn't come out of nowhere, but the video probably never would have made it on MTV. But it went up on YouTube, because there are no gatekeepers, and it got really huge. So it's giving a lot of artists who wouldn't have had that chance before the chance to really do something cool and make money off of it.

**Kyle Bylin/Apple**

When Apple Music launched in June of 2015, after a long wait and many rumors, it was basically Christmas for music tech nerds like Kyle and me. We fired up the podcast recorder and had a long chat about the much-anticipated streaming service.

KB: I'm sure everyone was paying attention when Zane Lowe went live on the air and started check-check-checking his mic, and people started listening in. So, Cortney, you and I were right there installed on our phones ready to tune in. What was your initial impression of Beats 1 Radio?

CH: I didn't understand why they were playing Brian Eno, and then there were some random bursts of Zane Lowe mic checking. I think it might have been a stunt of some sort, because his Twitter feed filled up, and he was retweeting people saying "Oh, I'm listening in Paris, I'm listening in Berlin, I'm listening in blah blah blah." I think if I was the average user who sort of clicked on Beats 1 Radio thinking "Oh, what is this, this sounds neat," I would have been confused and kind of put off by it. Yesterday was plagued by weird missteps, and I think that was probably a weird misstep.

KB: I don't think the average person would have understood that they were trying to build anticipation for when it actually went live on the air, and that this Brian Eno track that basically was the soundtrack to laying on the floor staring at the ceiling was interrupted by some UK guy going "Check, check, talking with a mic, hey, we ready, we hot, we ready to go." I mean, in all reality, and this is probably the reality, they probably just wanted to make sure that the station was working when they launched and that it was live, and they had no other option than to just – "We're just going to leave the thing on, nothing will break, it's working right now, the Apple correspondents in Mumbai say thumbs up, we can hear Zane, and we're just not going to touch it, otherwise we're afraid that the Beats Music 1 launch is just going to be a total flop if at zero hour it doesn't work."

CH: Yeah, I'm sure that that was a possibility. I do feel like they could have just played a playlist, or just played music – it just seemed weird to me. It seemed like part of a bigger problem, which is that the iTunes update for your laptop, or for your desktop, was not available yesterday. I think I got mine this morning. So, you know, on launch day you couldn't listen to it on your desktop, which I think is kind of a bad sign. Somebody was showing me last night if you click through a certain series of things, you get all these buttons, and none of the buttons were working. And again, I understand it's a new product, I understand there's always hiccups with new products, but on the other hand, it's Apple. You kind of expect a certain kind of buttoned-up-ness with Apple.

KB: Right. You would have expected a more polished launch, where the iOS update is available, it downloaded, Apple Music is ready to go, Beats 1 Radio is teed up and is playing some kind of a hip indie band that Zane really likes, and he's maybe kind of talking over the track like he was later, saying, like, "Hey, guys, we're just playing a couple of songs right now, get ready at 9 AM for the exclusive launch of Beats 1, we're going to be with you in a minute, just stand by." Right? It would have been so easy for him to do that. And furthermore, like you were saying, a lot of us, by the time 10 o'clock came around, especially for me, I went to my office. And I'm in my office, I'm at my Apple computer, it probably would have been nice to fire up the brand new version of iTunes and continue my music-listening experience that was taking place on my phone, and carry that over to the computer. That would have been a perfect opportunity to show off the ecosystem that you're part of as an Apple customer, and to get people tied into the fact that not only we're on your phone, we're on the desktop, we can do what Spotify can do just as good.

CH: Yeah, there's been weird connectivity issues for me, or weird portability issues. I saved an album that I've been meaning to listen to to a playlist, because I had to take the subway to a meeting this morning and I wanted something to listen to it while I was on the train, underground, disconnected. I started listening to the track, and as soon as I went underground and lost connection, the track stopped – I had to restart it. Then I get off the subway, walk up the stairs, get the connection back – the track stops again. I had to manually restart it. So is it the end of the world for me to have to take out my phone and hit the play button? Of course not. Is it kind of annoying and kind of silly and kind of glitchy? Yeah. And to Spotify's credit, I can listen to an offline cached album on Spotify whether I'm connected or not, it doesn't matter. So, you know, there's a lot of bugs, I think, that still need to be worked out here. They bought Beats over a year ago at this point. And Beats was a fully realized product. This was not an idea that someone was building and Apple bought it to build it. This was a product that was on the market and working, and Apple bought it and obviously made a lot of changes, but the fact that it's these little things – I'm just kind of like, "Ehh, I don't know." Again, it's a new product, I get it, but I kind of expected a little bit more polish.

KB: You know, I experienced weird things like that as well – something as simple as having to restart the Beats 1 station because it wasn't playing for some reason, or, yeah, a track I was playing – when it went to the next song, it didn't continue playing, and I was like "Oh, weird, what just happened," and I have to look at my phone, hit play again, be like "Oh, everything looks fine, maybe my phone glitched, was it Apple Music, I don't know." Another interesting thing that happened, though, on a related note, is: I have a 2013 Nissan Altima. In recent weeks, for some reason, when I plugged the USB-to-Apple connector into my phone, it didn't pull up the music on my phone. I was like "Oh, shit, did I break the USB connector, is something wrong?" I'd go in and have to connect through Bluetooth and then it would work. But when I got in my car on launch day, and I had Apple Music teed up, my car instantly recognized that I had an iPod plugged in – an iPhone – and started playing the music that I was listening to on the way to the car. It was like "Oh, this is not broken at all, this already integrates with my car. I'm just picking up where I left off." Whereas, sometimes Spotify doesn't always do that. For whatever reason, in my car, it still thinks my music device is an iPod, and it only plays well with Apple connected services. So if it's a podcast or music, it'll bring up what I'm listening to instantly, but if it's Spotify or otherwise, for some reason it doesn't have that level of integration.

CH: That's interesting. That's not something I've had to think about, but I think that's a good point. A lot of people are going to be listening to the radio in their car, especially if they're listening to Beats Radio, and yeah, the fact that it's a pretty seamless integration on your experience is great. I'm thinking about how this might compete with Sirius XM, and if it's a very seamless baked-in experience, that's going to be hard for Sirius XM to compete with.

KB: Well, and think of it this way, right: today we only have the one Beats 1 station with the 3 DJs all around the world or whatever, but if this is successful and there is an audience that gravitates towards this live radio programming, there's a high likelihood that they're going to expand the number of stations that they're offering, and these stations are being offered for free. Certainly they're going to take some amount of data, but if you're currently paying however much a month for Sirius XM radio, and now you have all these free Beats 1 radio stations available, maybe you're just going to be connecting to your phone and listening to those radio stations instead.

CH: Yeah, I think that's a possibility. I've been listening to Beats Radio a lot in the last 24 hours. I listened to it when I was running this morning, I listened to it when I was walking around earlier today, I was listening to it a lot yesterday as I was working and then out and about. So they have more than 3 DJs. The 3 DJs that they are been promoting are the main DJs, but they definitely have a bigger stable of DJs, so that's good, 'cause I would be worried about those 3 DJs just locked in a room forever. They also repeat shows; so Zane Lowe's show is on at 9 AM and 9 PM EST, for example, and it's the same show, so they have some repetition there. And then they also have the St. Vincent mixtape show, which I listened to a little bit and I actually found quite charming, because I like her and I liked the idea, and I liked the letter that she picked, and the whole thing that she did, and her playlist. It reminds me of a really good version of the indie channel on Sirius XM. But it is a huge mix of genres, and I think that's kind of new, at least in radio, which has traditionally been a very genre-driven format. I think that's why people like Sirius XM, is they can listen to a micro-genre. It's not even like the "Classic Rock" genre. My dad has Sirius XM, and it's not even like "I'm listening to the Classic Rock station," he listens to 60s on 6. That's all he listens to; it's a very set list of tracks and he's happy with that. And on Beats1, you would hear a hip-hop song, and then it would be the Rolling Stones, and then it would be something else. And then they had a countdown show that I was listening to this morning, which was interesting. It sounded like Casey Kasem, which I used to listen to when I was a kid, but it was unclear to me how the countdown was put together, if that makes any sense.

KB: Was it, maybe, the iTunes Music download chart? Apple has a ton of different charts that they could cobble together in order to make a countdown show.

CH: No, I'm sure it was one of those, it was never made clear which one of those it was. It wasn't like iTunes Top 20, you know, top 20 most downloaded tracks. Then I would have gotten it, but it's just like "This is the top 20 show, with such and such." I was like "top 20 what?" I mean, they were pop songs, Billboard Hot 100 type of stuff, but again, it was really sort of – we'll get into this later, but a lot of the things they say, like "top" and "hot" and "new", are very unclear as to why they are any of those things.

KB: I think that's definitely an interesting distinction. What does "new", "hot", "trending", "blogged about" mean in this context, especially when you're talking to essentially 100 countries at the same time? One of the bands might be extremely popular in one of those places but might not be established in another and vice versa. I mean, as we know, music often starts in one place and slowly spreads to another, so if you were on top of Macklemore and Ryan Lewis, that would have not been new music to a lot of the early adopters of that group, but once they went mainstream and "Thrift Shop" became a thing, then *everyone* knew what it was. It was no longer new, it was completely mainstream. You couldn't go anywhere without being exposed to it. My other understanding of the Beats Music stations is that they're in these hour-long blocks, right?

CH: Yeah.

KB: I think the theory there is: how long is a given person going to tune in, and to what extent can we then switch it up so that in every time zone we're going to be playing something new, that's current, that's interesting to them. We're not trying to make the rest of the world wake up with Los

Angeles, we're trying to have good content 24-7 that is reaching all of these different audiences at the times that they're most likely to enjoy it.

CH: Yeah, I mean, I think the Zane Lowe thing was 9 AM. I'm not 100% sure of this, but I think it was 9 AM and 9 PM EST. So I think that's how they're doing it, is that they just have – they have things airing twice a day. You're probably not going to be listening to both. I think a lot of radio programs air – NPR certainly airs the same shows sometimes multiple times, or if they're airing stories on the morning show, they'll air the same story every hour. There's a lot of repetition on radio, and that's fine. One thing that was weird is that there was a track played twice in a row, which was the Pharrell track. And I thought that was a very odd thing for him to have done. And that's generally a rule in radio that people don't break. You can play the same artist back to back, and someone did that this morning, but playing the same track twice in a row? I was like "Ok, that's weird."

KB: Yeah, for them to be repeating music on a station that doesn't need to is definitely a weird thing, right? 'Cause they don't have to conform to the same rules of traditional radio. They don't need to catch all of the people in their morning drive with the same Taylor Swift song. They can play whatever they want, as many songs as they want. Obviously they had to play the Pharrell "Happy" song more times than others, and they had to pay lip service to the fact that AC/DC was now on the service, but to repeat a song, or to repeat it twice in a row, that sounds kind of weird.

CH: Yeah, I mean, I was sort of annoyed by Zane Lowe, because after a while I was like "Ok, shut up." I am used to, now, radio being Pandora or Spotify Radio. I'm not used to DJs on my radio. So part of it is "Oh my god, why won't this guy stop talking." I get that it's the first day and that you're excited and live worldwide and yay, but, you know, I was listening this morning, and this guy Jordan had a show, and Jordan breaks in between tracks and is like "Oh, I was eating a brownie, and it was really good, and – " and I was like "I don't care? Sorry? Great?" Like – you know, it's almost a really really great version of college radio.

KB: The weird thing is, though, that everyone around the world has the capability of tweeting at the DJ while they're live on the air, so I'm sure a bunch of people locked into that are like "I'm eating a brownie too, that's so awesome!" or "Haha, brownies!" and they send a bunch of emoticons, right? That's the other weird thing about this experience, is that it's not just one radio station in one town, it's a radio station in 100 countries. And when you hear it through your earbuds on your phone, it's just a radio station, but then you look on Twitter and you're like "Whoa. There are people from everywhere that are listening to this." And if you follow Zane Lowe, he often retweets a lot of the things that are being tweeted to him.

CH: Yeah. Which is why I don't follow Zane Lowe.

KB: Oh, yeah, I'm sure that he's just blowing up Twitter all the time, especially when he's excited and on the air. But that's also an interesting dynamic, just this thing of – will Apple ever try to bring some of that activity inside of the show itself, or kind of make it more apparent that "Hey, here's the chat room that you can get into while you listen to the Zane Lowe show."

CH: Well, they are taking requests, and there was something where Jaden Smith requested a song and it got played, and that was big on Twitter, so yeah – they're taking requests, which, I think, is kind of interesting, again, because it's this very old-school – it's a really interesting mashup of the really old-school radio stuff, which is really DJ-driven, DJ-personality-driven, multiple-genre, you know, request-driven to a certain extent, you know, very social. Again, sort of informal, very chatty, with this newer – with the fact that it's streaming. So they've actually taken a product that's very old and they're like "Ok, we're putting this on the Internet." I don't think it's new that there's people listening to the same thing all over the world. BBC Radio, you can listen to in any number of countries. I don't think you're going to be interacting with it, maybe, as much, but I've listened to KCRW in many different countries, because I have the KCRW app and I really like it. So it's totally possible for someone in Cape Town or Tokyo or Buenos Aires to have the KCRW app, tweet at Jason Bentley and be like "Hey, man, that was an awesome track." So it's not a totally new thing, but maybe Apple is really selling that. "This is worldwide radio," Zane kept yelling.

KB: "World Wide Live Radio, Zane Lowe here."

CH: Yeah.

KB: Something that I thought of as we were talking, is that a few years ago I actually had a short internship at a local radio station in Fargo, North Dakota, and me being the little whip-smart kid who's reading all the books about the downfall of the music business, I'm like "Oh, traditional radio's dying, no one wants to call in and request songs anymore," and he's like "Dude, high school students won't stop calling us. They call and request songs *all of the time.*" And it was just like "What?" He's like "Dude, getting your song played on the radio is still a thing that younger people are still engaged with. This is happening."

CH: Yeah. It's kind of crazy. I remember doing that when I was in high school, which is kind of a long time ago. But yeah, I mean, I think people are excited about that. Maybe people were interested in – still are interested in – Pandora and Spotify and this very, very lean-back radio because they – because a lot of commercial radio has become a) kind of abysmal and b) completely depersonalized. So, you know, if most of your local radio stations are either the JACK FM shuffler format or somebody syndicated from halfway across the country, you can't really call in to your local radio station if it's the type of station that's just syndicated programs, right? There's no local interaction, there's no local activity. So maybe this is sort of what people have been searching for for a while. Maybe it's not that people necessarily wanted this really impersonal radio, it's that you didn't have an option, right? Radio had gone so far in the direction of everything's impersonal, programmed by robots out of Clear Channel World HQ, wherever that is, that this is now sort of the DJ-driven multi-genre format is super old, at least in the US. In other countries, I think, it's more relevant, certainly in commercial radio. Like, I guess KCRW, to a certain extent, does it, but they sort of stay within one lane and don't venture too far out.

KB: You know, I think I've got this figured out. At some point some guy named Chris in Ohio is going to call the hotline and say "Hey, I'd really love you to play this Guns N Roses song, 'Sweet Child O' Mine', I'd also just love you to send this song out to my girlfriend, I'd like to ask her to marry me. Sara, if you're listening right now, this song is for you, I love you." And if Zane Lowe plays the clip of this guy requesting this song and asking his girlfriend to marry him, it's much different than your local radio station doing something cheesy. This is the entire world watching, and it's going to blow up on all the news outlets – "Guy Asks Girl To Marry Him On Beats 1 Radio."

CH: It's viral, right? Again, so, the "Jaden Smith requested Blah Blah Blah track". That immediately went viral, because it's Jaden Smith, but yeah, I can see other interesting viral moments happening on this. I think it's also interesting to see where the requests are coming from. So it's kind of cool if it's like "Oh, here's a request from Lagos, here's a request from Kuala Lumpur, here's a request from blah blah blah." That's going to be super interesting. You know, they say worldwide, and I guess technically it's in 100 countries, so that's pretty far on the way there, but their offices are London, New York, LA. That doesn't feel as worldwide to me. That feels very Western, very English-speaking. Everything is in English. All of the DJs are speaking in English, all of the songs that I heard are in English. That's kind of a bummer. And maybe there are going to be subchannels of Beats 1 Radio France, Beats 1 Radio Russia, Beats 1 Radio whatever, but – again, it comes back to this idea again of "We're worldwide, but." But you gotta speak English to listen.

KB: Right, well, I mean – there are many countries that love bands that don't even know the words or vice versa, right?

CH: Totally.

KB: So-and-so group is the biggest group ever in this country, and you're like "Wait, how is that even possible." So the Western world has influenced the developed world, or however you want to look at it. I think a really important question right now, Cortney, is – are we missing the Eminem interview right now? I feel like that was supposed to air sometime today, and I feel like we missed it.

CH: You know what's interesting is – I don't know. And I didn't see anything on any of my socials about it. I also didn't get a push notification about it. I haven't seen anything.

KB: Right, maybe – I feel like it's supposed to be sometime today. So I am personally kind of excited about the notion of Eminem being interviewed on Beats 1 Radio by Zane Lowe because I hear Zane Lowe is a great interviewer, I think obviously Eminem is obviously a very relatable character that all of us grew up hearing his story about his mom and his wife and Haley – he's like the sitcom that played out on an album, except for the sitcom was a psychopathic killer who happens to be a white DJ, or white rapper, if you will. But I think what'll be very interesting is when you have Eminem live on the radio, and everyone is tweeting about what he's saying, everyone's tweeting at Eminem, headlines are coming out about the thing Eminem revealed about his new album, or his new partnership with Dre, or whatever it is – Eminem can announce things on this radio station. He knows everyone is paying attention right now. Especially the media has close eyes on Beats 1 Radio. And I think going forward, when other major artists come on this station, the media has to pay attention. What if Britney Spears says something? We need to know about it, because it's our job to write blog posts about what Britney Spears says. Right? So that alone is just going to continue to drum up attention for Beats 1 Radio, because there's a whole rotating cast of interesting artists and really passionate fans. Like, come on, One Direction is just going to break Beats 1 Radio and the phone is just going to turn into a brick.

CH: Oh, no, they totally are. Zayn and Zane together!

KB: Ok, now you're getting too zany, Cortney.

CH: Well, I mean, yeah, I'm assuming the Eminem thing hasn't happened just because my Twitter feed isn't blowing up, but I didn't see it advertised anywhere in the app. I didn't hear any ads for it when I was listening this morning. I don't know! That's one thing that, again, they have to work out is – they kept saying go check the website for the schedule, which, fine, I get it, you don't want to sit here and recite the schedule when you could be playing music, but a little more attention – "And then we've got such and such coming up, followed by such and such."

KB: I mean, this is giving them too much credit, but they're going to be able to set Calendar Alerts at some point if that ends up being the most requested feature.

CH: Yeah.

KB: Send me a Calendar Alert when the Eminem show is going to air! What's that? We make the calendar on your phone! Right? The level of integration, if they really wanted to do it, could be that deep.

CH: Yeah, I mean, I think that's the next thing that they can get to. Calendar Alerts, putting a show on your calendar, all of the stuff that they have their tentacles into on your phone already, you know, looking at what kind of – what does your calendar look like? Are you really busy one day, or do you have a chill day? Ok, if you have a chill day, we'll play music that's more chill. If you have a crazy busy day where you have like 20 meetings, maybe you want music to pump you up in the morning! You know, that's just sort of one somewhat clunky example, but maybe your calendar's full of therapist appointments, so they give you a tearful playlist.

KB: What you're reminding me of is the WNYC radio app. What you can kind of do is that I've have 45 minutes, I'm interested in these topics, I know about these shows, go! And it instantly creates a 45-minute radio block customized for you to consume. I'd have to imagine at some point this would be a sick feature that Apple could do, where you're just like "Give me 35 minutes of music," and "Make it from the For You section, maybe add a little bit of new, add that short block with Dre earlier, whatever." They can have customized blocks of music and radio on a whole other level, 'because they have 10,000 playlists that they can pull from and string together based on how much time you have to engage with the service, or how long your given commute is. It's really kind of quirky to say, but imagine it's integrated with your calendar and Apple Maps, and as soon as your garage door closes, the last song ends, and you're like "Whoa."

CH: Yeah, I mean, that's incredible. It can – if it can integrate with Apple Maps, which is kind of a terrible product, but let's say Apple Maps gets fixed and becomes good, one thing that would be really interesting – and this is kind of riffing – is – you know, I've been going out of town this summer, and driving up to different places on the weekends, and the traffic is always abysmal on Friday evenings in New York. It's just terrible and stressful and horrible. And if it can say "Ok, it looks like you're trying to get out of New York, because you've entered directions to the Catskills, and we can see from the traffic reports that it's terrible, we're going to play you some really chill music to de-stress you." And then it can read like "Oh, you're going for a day drive in the Catskills, because you've mapped this out, and you're cruising on the open road, let's play music for that." I want an app that I open and I push a button and it plays what I want. Apple Music is kind of the opposite of that. That's not to say that they couldn't do something like that. And I want to go back to WNYC for a minute, because this is something I loved in the radio section was that WNYC is streaming in there. ESPN is streaming in there. As far as I can tell those are the only 2 non-music stations, but, again, I think that's awesome. I was like "Apple should buy iheartradio, and then all your radio is in one place."

KB: I think that's the definition of monopoly, is that owning the largest radio conglomerate in the United States.

CH: Yeah. Anti-trust, schmanti-trust.

KB: Then you really would have every DJ promoting this iPhone.

CH: Ok, so that probably breaks some anti-trust laws. Ok, every antitrust law. But –

KB: Ok. Let's step back from Apple buying iheartmedia and step towards something we discussed before, which is Apple buys Gimlet Media; now Startup Podcast, Mystery Show and Reply All are exclusive to iTunes Radio, excuse me, now they're exclusive to Apple Music Radio, and they basically say "Ok, Alex Blumberg, we need 15 more shows from you. How many more staff do you need to create the next Serial," and Alex Bloomberg names the highest number that he can think of, and they're just like "Sure. Go hire all your friends. Radiotopia? Bring them in too. Whatever." Like, chump change to Apple to bring the best radio producers, podcast creators, public radio hosts all into one place, to create this content that is normally tied to donations and stuff. But if

Apple decides that Serial and This American Life are going to sell phones and get people really excited about using phones, of course they're going to do that. Why wouldn't they?

CH: Yeah, that's interesting. So the Podcasts app, which I never use, is not very good. They definitely need to fix that. But yeah. That's potentially another interesting way to get an audience, because there are probably a lot of people who aren't as into music as they are into podcasts. Or – I like to listen to both, I like to go back and forth and toggle back and forth. And, you know, being able to – even just being able to subscribe to podcasts at Apple Music and then control your playlist that way.

KB: Give me a little bit of talk, little bit of music.

CH: Yeah. Like, I want to hear this – I want to hear Serial, and then I want to hear, you know, this new playlist about this, and then I want to hear murder ballads. Yeah, haha. One that's, to me, interesting, is – I'm starting to move away from segmenting content, not just by genre but by format. And there's no reason that you can't have everything in Apple Music. You can't have podcasts, and talk, I mean, they've got ESPN Radio, but other radio channels. I feel like the more they can control, the better it's going to be for them.

KB: I feel like in this moment it's important to say something like "Cortney, stop trying to build iTunes inside Apple Radio. It's already kind of confusing and cluttered. Stop trying to turn Apple Music into iTunes, right?"

CH: But I'm not!

KB: Spotify recently put podcasts and videos in their app, and it fit in kind of nice. I think the challenge, though, is – it's already complicated the way it is to zero in on the music you want to hear. Adding podcasts would be its own kind of animal. That said, there would be a way to do it, and it could be interesting. I just wanted to  point out that given what we have today, where Apple Music stands, us talking about adding podcasts into Apple Music itself – I mean, it could work, and it could work very well – Intro to Serial, Intro to Moth, or whatever. Collections of podcasts?

Ooh, that gets interesting. However, it is just worth at least putting the footnote there, saying maybe at some point, but hopefully not today. We have to remember that Apple acquired the lovely startup name Swell, and eventually that technology should find its way to the Podcast app itself. I mean, Apple's not dumb. They know that they're the chief proprietors of podcasting. I hope they realize that their podcasting app isn't that great and that eventually they turn it into a Pandora-style radio station that recommends you the best podcasts based on the ones you've been listening to the most. You take away the subscriber model, you take away all the episodic content - play me something great right now and I'll hook into the story. And you can do that with stories more easily than you can do it with music. Because let's be real, not everyone likes a specific song, but everyone loves stories.

CH: Right. I guess, for me, because of the way I consume playlists – I consume podcasts, I'm a little different in that I have a couple podcasts that I like, I listen to every day, for me – you know, the way that I'm listening to music – and podcasts, which I realize is somewhat specific to me, is that I like playlists of podcasts. So if I'm on a 20 mile run, the last thing I want to do is stop and get my phone out because a podcast ended and I want to go to the next one, or I want to be able to set it up so for the first part of my run I listen to an interesting podcast, and then I listen to music for a little bit, and then I listen to a different podcast. Depending on what I'm doing, to have that scheduled seamlessly would be really great. Now, you know, again, I'm probably a fairly unique use case. Not many people go on 20 mile runs regularly. But I do think there are a lot of people where – and this gets to another problem I was having with Beats 1, which is, and again, I'm a unique use case, I was listening to it on my run, and I was like "Oh, I really like this song, I really like this song." And I have no way to come back to the song. So I can't say – I have to take my phone out. I have to be like "Oh, this is such and such." And that's probably not clear to me how I save that artist, how I move forward with that artist. You know, how do I follow that artist, how do I find their other stuff. I think there's probably a way to do that, but it's very in-app. So when people are listening to radio a lot of the time, they're in the car, so you probably shouldn't be using your phone, or they're out and about. It's a little hard to sort of make that connection right now with Beats 1.

KB: Yeah, it is kind of this weird notion that on your lock screen there's a heart, so you can heart it, but when you do that, it doesn't go in your Library, and to my knowledge it doesn't go in your profile. Maybe there's a hearted playlist that they'll start for you at some point. Obviously Spotify had the star system before. But you're right. Is there a quick way to heart, favorite, add the current song that you're hearing on Beats 1 Radio and put it in a place where you know where it went so you can find it later. The other thing I think you're talking about is just the notion that in any given interaction within Apple Music, when you click the menu for the song, I've seen some menus that took up over half the screen and had at least eight options under them. I'm just like "Whoaaaa." Who let eight options float up on an onscreen menu? You can do anything you want with this! Just try it now.

CH: Let's talk about the option paralysis, because I think we've talked about the radio stuff, and maybe we can talk about the other section, which is the New section. And the New section is, for me, the definition of "There are so many options, what am I going to do." So the New section – you get, you know, at least under All Genres, which is what I have it set to. You get, first of all, the top thing is Taylor Swift's 1989, which is – hahaha. You know. Screw you, Spotify, I guess. That sort of scrolls across and you get a ton of different options there. Then you've got New Music, which is a bunch of albums that came out this week. Because it's all genres, it's all the stuff, none of it is customized for your specific tastes. Then you get Hot Tracks. Then you get Recent Releases. And by the way, 1989 came out last year. The AC/DC album came out many years ago. And then Leon Bridges came out relatively recently, so I guess that's fine.

KB: But no one on a streaming music service has heard it before!

CH: That's true.

KB: It is new to streaming music users.

CH: It is recent for streaming music. Ok, fair enough. Then you get Top Songs, which, ok. Top Songs and Hot Tracks. I guess there's a difference? It's not clear to me what that difference is.

KB: Because if it's a Top Song, wouldn't it also be hot?

CH: Yeah. You know, listen, I'm sure it's based on some algorithm. I'm unclear what it is. And then you get Hot Albums, and then you get Discovered On Connect Audio. I can kinda figure out what that is, but I don't know what that is. It's not clear to me.

KB: I think it's – you're right that it's really obfuscated. Being the experts that we are, I think it is music that these artists have uploaded to Connect, and now they're surfacing it to you in the New section, like, people are discovering the Zedd ID demo V5 instrumental. That's very SoundCloud-y of you.

CH: Yeah. I almost feel like – that's the best you've got? Not to be mean, but...

KB: This is how you're leveraging the brand you service that everyone's really excited about? ID Demo V5?

CH: Christ, at least frigging Tidal could get Alicia Keys exclusives.

KB: The B side of the B side.

CH: Yeah. It's like, these are just really random things. And then it's -

KB: But Cortney, keep scrolling! Songza comes right up next.

CH: Yeah. Keep scrolling. Then you've got Apple Music editors, their playlists. And then you've got a million different options. Activities, a million different options. Curators? Ok, they've got Rolling Stone, fine. They've got Vogue as a curator? Ok. And then Discovered On Connect Video.

KB: Yeah, I have no idea what that is.

CH: And then Recommended Music Videos, which, hey, look, there's Pharrell. And then you've got Summertime Playlists. Ok. And then you've got New Artists. And then you've got Alternative Essential, and you can click through that, and there's more to click through. If you click on Alternative Essentials, you have this endless scroll of albums. It is TOO MUCH. So you wind up – I wind up just scrolling and scrolling and just being like "I can't even deal with this." And I'm a crate digger. I like just going to record stores. I like digging for music. I like playlists. I like discovery. I've been in the music business for ten years – and even I'm like "Oh my god, this is way too much." And then – I'll use my sister as the test case. I imagine my sister looking at this and being like "No. This is too hard. I'm going to go listen to Pandora, because Pandora, I type in blah blah blah artist, and I hit a button."

KB: It's kind of like they designed all the other tabs, and they're like "How do we fit in everything else inside this tab?" I would think that you can have the Apple Music editors, activities and curators at the top of the page. I think slightly below that could be recent releases, or new tracks, or a mix of both. And then maybe a chart or two. And then, only then, you have the essentials, a specific playlist that kind of maybe fits into the time of year or something like that – but they're trying to cram so much into this page that it could be an app in and of itself. And many of these are apps in and of themselves, right? Like, the curated section is Songza, the connect is SoundCloud, the videos are Vevo, the hot tracks, if we're being specific, is Twitter Music. There's just so much going on here. And then the essentials is, I think, is really interesting because it's almost like "Hey, in addition to all this music, we've also installed the greatest album deep dive that you can think of in this given category." And I'm looking at it and I'm like "Oh, that's right. These are all really excellent records that I should probably listen to or know about" – that maybe if you were just opening up for the first time you wouldn't think of playing.

CH: But here's the thing. The word essentials then becomes kind of meaningless. I know that's a semantics kind of argument to trot out, but essential is kind of unique, in a way, where everyone's like "Such and such is unique!" I'm like "No, it's not." How essential can an album be when it's one of 300 albums that you sit there and scroll through. I don't know! I mean, they're all good albums – what does essential even mean. I know that's a very nitpicky linguistic-y thing for me to say, but if I'm going to – I want the essentials, that means I want a very small digestible selection of something, that doesn't mean I want a hundred albums that I have to scroll through and pick one.

KB: It's almost like they added a record store at the bottom just for good taste.

CH: The people who built this service, essentially, are musicians and music industry people, and they're really incredibly smart, and they're really incredibly hardworking, and they are passionate about music. And they're the people who would love this type of stuff, right? They're crate diggers. I can think of nothing that would be more fun than going crate digging with Trent Reznor, or with Dr. Dre, or with Dave Allen, or Ian Rogers, or Jimmy Iovine, even though he might kill you. But not – the vast majority of people are not crate diggers. The vast majority of people would go into Academy Records and would be like "What is happening." Right? There's a reason that Tower Records kind of went under and you started getting people going to Target for records, because Target had a very small sort of curated selection.

KB: You know, they wouldn't be going inside the store to say what is happening, they'd be like "I'm looking for the one album, I think it has a blue cover, I think there's a horse in the name? Maybe an animal of some kind? It kind of sounds like that one band from Hype Machine, but I'm not really sure." And the store clerk is just like "Oh, my god, you abysmal human being, let me find you that shitty record that you like."

CH: Yeah, that's true. And, look, 90% of the people who went to Tower Records went to buy whatever was #1 that week. They got in, they got out. And Tower Records obviously had everything that was going to sell a lot right up front. And you could go crate dig if you wanted, but it was really just like – most people were just like "Ok, N Sync album, here, done." And, again, the For You section, which is the first section that a lot of people see after you hit those stupid bubbles, is, again, a lot of the stuff in there I like, and I'm like "Oh, I want to listen to this, this is cool," but every time you refresh it you get a bunch more stuff. And, it again feels like – how am I ever going to get through this? There's a zillion playlists I want to listen to. Option paralysis. Here's 50 cool things – how do I even attempt to get through this?

KB: One album at a time, Cortney.

CH: Yes.

KB: I will say, though, the For You section, we talked about this, it's pretty goddamned good.

CH: Yeah, it's awesome. Mine – my picks are like – I got Post-Rock Afternoon. I've got a bunch of Sonic Youth stuff. I've got a bunch of Elliott Smith deep cuts, which is like, oh my god, this is really, really good stuff. But, again, I can't just keep scrolling and keep scrolling. This is just days and days and days of music that I want to keep listening to.

KB: And I think they're hoping for that, right?

CH: Yeah.

KB: I think it's an interesting challenge, because everyone gets lost in this idea of "We have 30 million songs." But Apple is really saying "We have the 50 albums that you want." And every time you refresh you're like "Oh, that's right, the Black Parade album by My Chemical Romance, I'd love to listen to that!" It's somewhere in my collection in the music spreadsheet, if you will, but when I see that I'm like "Yeah, I'd listen to that!" And that's what's so intriguing about this. It's not the hottest newest albums. It's like – "We think you're going to like Sum 41, Underclass Hero, it came out in 2007, we think you might click play." And I think there's something to be said for the fact that they know these things about you based on what you bought or favorited, and they're playing things that you might not think in your head, like, "I'm looking for Blood Sugar Sex Magik by Red Hot Chili Peppers right now. The only thing that's going to make my day is a little blood, sugar, sex and magik." But when you see it, the iconic cover and everything, you're like "Ooh, what is that, it's interesting, let me click on it, I haven't heard that in forever." It really does have that kind of nostalgia to it, and it has that "Oh, what can I listen to," and you're like "Oh, a ton of good stuff is here."

Which is interesting to contrast this, by the way, with – the For You section is great and the New section is just a shitshow.

CH: The For You – again, I'm looking at it, I'm scrolling through mine, I'm like "Oh my god, yeah, that Jesus Lizard record I haven't heard in forever, I love that record!" Or there's a Boredoms record, or there's a Pussy Galore record that's really old. I'm like "Oh my god, these are all things that I listened to at one point that I haven't listened to in ages." I probably wouldn't have gone back and been like "Yeah, I want to hear Pussy Galore right now," but now I'm like "Yeah, I really wanna hear that! That's awesome!"

KB: Here's my question – had they customized the New section kind of like the For You section, would it be overwhelming, because you'd just be like "Oh my god, all the new music by my favorite artists! Here are the hot tracks, here are the recent releases." I think that'd be an entirely different experience. That isn't to say that it's still not a shitshow and that there still aren't too many options, but had it been personalized, that becomes something different, right? 'cause it's not all this stuff that you're unfamiliar with. It's not the Spotlight on Sia, it's like – here's the spotlight on the new Fort Minor song that came out. We saw you favorited Linkin Park, by the way, Mike Shinoda is kinda getting back in the groove again. You're like "Ooh, that's a song I've been meaning to listen to, I read about it online." You know, that gets into a whole other world of – music services aren't that great about telling you when artists you like put out more music.

CH: Yeah. So with the New section, you can sort by genre, which does narrow things down a little bit, right? Your default is All Genres, and that's the page that's endless scrolling with a billion options. But I just set it to Indie, and it was a little bit more manageable. It's still a bunch of charts and spotlights and squares and rectangles and all that, but it's a little less overwhelming. But you're right. I mean, that's – one of the things that I find is that I miss new stuff all the time. Because unless people I know are telling me about it, I don't know that so-and-so's putting something out. And there are a lot of artists who aren't that great on social media. Yeah, I miss stuff all the time. So again, I feel like there's room in there for more notifications. There's room in there for

"Oh, yeah, so and so put something out, so and so's doing this." We haven't even gotten to talking about, again, the fact that Apple's a really walled garden, and how great would it be if it was like, they had some sort of AmEx presale for Apple Music subscribers. So they'd send you a push notification that's like "Sleater-Kinney tickets go on sale tomorrow, do you want in." Something like that. Like, that, to me, would increase the stickiness tenfold. 'Cause you're like "Oh, I get all these cool deals." Just to talk about the Connect feature a little bit, that feels very very undercooked, and the content that I'm seeing on the Connect features is not, kind of not great. And I feel like you can only ask artists for so much music content before it just a) goes everywhere else, like we've seen with what Tidal was doing, or b) it's so dumb that it's kind of like "Oh, why am I sticking around – FKA Twigs is practicing her choreography, this video that's on her Connect page." I'm like "That's nice, I kind of don't care." And again, it's one of those things where – you know, then you have a problem with a lot of bands like Sonic Youth. Oh, I get this weird live track from ten years ago as my Sonic Youth exclusive. Again, I don't care. And Sonic Youth's not around! And the two principals in the band hate each other's guts! Now what are you going to do. I feel like there's a way to make Connect stickier that's not the same old "Here's some exclusive content! Here's a live demo!" It's just like "Eh."

KB: What's weird though is that, for example, in my Connect feed I'm seeing that Eminem posted this Phenomenal music film teaser. I'm like "Ok, I have no idea what that is." I know Phenomenal is one of his new songs, but there are 9589 hearts and there are 1484 comments. And, you know, just for posterity, let's read them. "This is cool, and the interview is great. I like this song. Eminem can't act. This looks bad. You are the best at rapping and I'm a huge fan of your work, and you're a – ooh, what does that say, asshole? Love the song! What's up people! Brilliant!" But this is interesting, right? This is the feed of mainstream America going "Eminem! Eminem!"

CH: Yeah. No matter what you put out there, there's gonna be a bunch of people liking it, commenting on it, being like "This is cool, yay!" I just feel like it's – right now Connect does not feel like it adds that much value to me. There's a way they could add value, but they're not doing it right now. And they're still, again, getting to the bigger problem, which is

– there are a lot of bands out there right now that don't have that much to connect to. It's either stuff that's really old, no one cares about, they're too obscure. You know, I obviously –

KB: Let's be real, though. I have friends who are paid to update the social media accounts of dead musicians. There are entire firms of people who make sure that the Van Morrison page is well populated with sticky, interesting content. These are problems that get solved pretty quick.

CH: You know, that's right. I mean, listen - most artists that are artists who have been around for any amount of time have a vault of stuff. I mean, The Doors have been releasing stuff for 40 years now.

KB: Just wait until Tupac joins Connect.

CH: Oh my god. But again, it's like, how many Doors B-sides and re-releases and – again, I know there's kind of an endless appetite for some of this stuff, but, you know, are people really going to care that here's a demo from 20 years ago that we dug out of our vault? And there are some completists, but I don't know how many.

KB: Right, I mean, I don't know. This is a kind of interesting to point to raise, right? Which is – I agree the field feels kind of half-baked right now. Right now I don't really have that compelling of content. But one can imagine that as music videos are debuted in the feed, and exclusive songs, that it's going to pick up some amount of traction if high-value stuff like that is starting to surface. And I think, like you said before, like, the following model, and how to get more artists in this page – isn't clear right now, or as clear as it should be. Apparently I just figured it out live, that on the upper left hand corner of the Connect feed there's this little head, and then you go to the Following part, and under 'Find More Artists and Curators' you can see who you're all following. And I think – there it is – you can find a list of Recommended people.

CH: Oh, I didn't get a Recommended list, I just got a list of who I was following. Half of them I'm not sure why I was following.

KB: Yeah, if you look at – under Find More Artists and Curators, Carrie Underwood, Foo Fighters – the list is very short, though, which hints to me that maybe not a lot of artists are not actually connected up, which would be its own interesting headline. Like, why isn't this fully populated with every single artist that is in my collection or available on iTunes Music right now. Where's Pharrell? Why am I not being recommended to follow Pharrell as the first person I was alerted about?

CH: Yeah, or why aren't these pages sort of somewhat built, pulling from All Music Guide, or pulling from any other source. Even if it's a band that's really obscure that's been broken up for 10 years, or Elliott Smith, dead for 10 years – ok, I can still follow him and get some sort of a page that's like, got like, here are some photos, here are some songs, here's a bio. Ok, I'm following him and maybe it'll get updated. But it seems weird that what's recommended is someone I have no connection to or affinity for. They've done such a good job of recommending stuff to me in terms of the For You section, that's really great stuff. And then I'm getting recommended One Direction and Maroon 5, which is completely outside the scope of something that I'm interested in.

KB: I mean, as a willing reporter and research participant, you really should follow One Direction just to see what happens.

CH: Zayn on Zane.

KB: Let's get zany.

CH: Let's get zany! Let's make Zayn puns the rest of the day.

KB: But yeah, so that covers Connect, we've talked about the New section, we've talked about For You, we've talked about Radio. My Music is pretty straightforward, it just has your most recently added albums or songs, and then there's this sorting function where you can search by the artists, albums or songs in your collection. And then if you swipe, which is its own kind of mechanic, it's like – you can swipe, you can click, you can filter, there's a lot of UI here. But mix it up, find some great playlists for you, or make your own here. Oh, wow, and it's like "Add a title, add songs." Can I Genius this? I don't think I can.

CH: Yeah, and the thing we also haven't talked about is the bubbles.

KB: Oh, the bubbles.

CH: The bubbles. So they got rid of the sentence, which is good. Apparently the scuttlebutt inside Apple is that Trent Reznor really fought for the sentence, 'because that was his baby, but they killed it, so maybe we'll get an angry song about that in a few years. Somehow I don't think so.

KB: Bow down to the Apple you deserve.

CH: Yeah, somehow Trent's just like "I'm gonna take my pile of money and go back to my castle and I'm just gonna let it slide." But who knows, maybe once he's fully vested we'll get some angry tweets. But yeah, they kept the bubbles.

KB: Yeah, instead of the sentence we just have the paragraph, which is the New section.

CH: Yeah. So the bubbles – user experience with the bubbles, again – for me was confusing, and I'm someone who knows about this stuff. So I can't imagine being Joe Average on the street and being like "So, I need to click the bubbles that I like and double click the bubbles that I don't like." And what am I doing? It was very, very - I was like "Why don't they just have a list of genres? Why did they have to get clever and cute and make bubbles? They're clever and they're cute and it serves the same purpose as if users just rolled over some genres and picked some." So, yeah, I just thought the bubbles were kind of weird. And then you get more bubbles, and then you're finally done with the bubbles.

KB: The other weird thing about the bubbles was like – I feel like when we did the bubbles on Beats Music that the artists I was being recommended were so glaringly obvious that you almost had to click them anyways. And some of the bubbles here, I'm like "Who the hell is that? Why is that bubble being recommended?" And I kind of coyly thought "Did someone pay to have a bubble?"

CH: That actually brings us to a whole other interesting topic, which is – you know, it is not transparent at all how stuff appears in streaming services. This is not just an Apple problem, or an Apple Music problem – this is a bigger issue, I guess, not a problem. But when you look at who is on playlists, or who is featured on these pages, I think that people have this expectation that it's organic, or that it's an editor picking it, but don't forget, people paid for endcaps when there were record stores. You didn't just get your album on the endcap if the record store owner thought you were neat. You got it because you put money in it. One thing that I have yet to hear anyone really talk about is – what is the financial situation in terms of getting your stuff on playlists? Getting your stuff in a bubble? Getting your stuff at the top of the screen? Does Beats Radio abide by the same rules as terrestrial radio when it comes to payola, or not? Is online radio that is not just machine learning governed by the same payola rules? Could I just buy a bunch of spots on iTunes, or on Beats Radio, if I'm a label?

KB: The funny thing that's kind of emerging in my mind is this kind of notion that - we all know the picture of the old record school guy going to the local DJ – "Got some tickets? Want some tickets to the show? You want baseball tickets? What's the deal here?" But when you have the record industry guy or the radio promoter guy going to the Apple Music curator: "Oh, I could use a new Tesla! That could maybe work! What about those Google Glasses? Get me an explorer pair, and we'll think about putting your playlist on." These aren't people who are your kind of lowly but happy and excited DJ, these are employers of the largest corporation in the world, and they're being paid really well, I would imagine.

CH: Well, a) we don't know. Right? B) – I mean, b) look how many investment bankers did incredibly stupid things because 1 million dollars a year wasn't enough, they wanted 10 million dollars. You know? There are plenty of people who are well paid who still take bribes and still do stupid shit. And c) well, Zane Lowe probably does pretty well for himself. But a lot of these lists are put together by people who are editorial curators who might not make that much money, they might be freelancers – Apple was hiring a ton of freelancers to put together a lot of these lists. I mean, if you're a freelance – and I say this as someone who was a freelance music writer – you don't make a lot of money. And, again, I don't know any of this, I'm not accusing anyone of this, I'm just sort of thinking aloud here – what's to say – basically, what are the rules governing this? How editorially independent are these lists?

KB: I mean, the first joke I was going to make was like "So, kids, there's this thing called greed, and there's this thing called money, and when you have a lot of influential people who are very greedy, and want money, they exchange goods in order to get services, often music placements in one of the world's largest streaming services to date, or soon, right?" I read online that someone called Apple Music Jimmy Iovine's wet dream, right? Because now you owned the radio station, now you owned the streaming service, now you don't have to worry about all the behind-the-doors dealing of getting the radio promoter to go to the radio station or anything, you're just like "Oh, yeah, that's right, my 30 guys that I hired are curating all this music for us. If my buddy Doug Morris puts in a phone call and needs the new song as part of the new music playlist on the front page, I'm going to pick up the phone."

CH: Yeah, there's never – look, I mean, I've been in that world, in the edit side of things. None of it's pure, right? There were crappy artists that I wrote about because their publicist repped a good artist that I wanted to write about later. I never took bribes, but none of it's ever that pure. But then again, money never exchanged hands, right? I think what I'm curious about is – and again, this is not solely Apple Music's problem, or Apple Music's issue, it's – what are the rules governing this? Because that's really unclear. And I think a lot of people have this idea that "Oh, stuff gets played on radio 'because it's really good," which is not true at all, as anyone who has ears knows, but it's almost a weird competitive disadvantage if you are on terrestrial radio and you can't accept something that you put on streaming radio.

KB: Well, Cortney, I think those are excellent points, and I think this concludes our extra extra special Apple Music edition. Do you have any final thoughts you'd like to share about the service or any of the feedback you've seen online?

CH: Yeah, again, I like Beats 1 Radio a lot, I'll probably continue to listen to it. I like the service. I think it's better than Spotify. It's not exactly what I'm looking for, but I also always kind of go back to 10 years ago, or even seven years ago, when we had smartphones, if you had said to me "There's an app where all the music in the world is on this app and you can listen to it any time and only pay one monthly fee," I'd be like "Holy shit, that's the greatest thing ever, this changes everything." And now I'm sitting here with that app several times over in my hand and I'm being like "I don't really like the layout, there's too many playlists –" So, like, listen. I'm very aware that streaming music and the fact that we have these apps is an incredible thing. But I mean – first you get something and you criticize the hell out of it, so. I think my final thought is, I've got and I'll keep using it, I've got my free trial, in three months I'll see.

KB: You know, I'm on the same page. 1) I called my book Promised Land, because this whole concept occurred to me, which is that had you went back in time to young Little Kyle and said "Look, look! There's this thing called an iPhone, with Spotify, and it'll play all the music you want forever." You're like "Whoa! It's like torrents, but in my phone!" You're like "No, no, no – there's no downloading. You're streaming." You're just like "What, that's insane! I don't have to download anything? It's only this much per month? Here's my 9 dollars!" But when – as you grow up, and you are paid to have thoughts on Apple Music – well, let's be real, no one pays us to have these thoughts, but – when you grow up and have thoughts about Apple Music, you're like "This isn't as good as it could be," or "This page and this navigation is weird." And you – because you have this perspective on what this means or could mean, it kind of takes away from the whole enjoyment that you could have and the excitement about it. But at the same time we both giddily read through our For You section and were like "There's more music here to listen to than I know what to do with!" I had a similar thought. I think that's more than I can really say about where Spotify has taken their service, which is that it's extremely playlist-centric, it's based on time of day and particular activity and mood. And I understand that this is how the populace thinks about music, but at the same time – surfacing the right records at the right moment can get someone excited to listen to the music from their high school year or any number of other seminal things. And I think if anything, Apple is hitting on that and hitting on it well, especially in the For You section.

CH: Yeah. Again, Apple Music is pretty good. I listened to Beats 1 Radio this morning and I was like "This is great. They're playing really interesting stuff." I didn't like all of it, obviously, but I liked a lot of it. The St. Vincent thing was so charming and so fun and really well done, and I was just like "This is great. This is really awesome." Part of my – one of my complaints about Spotify is that Spotify is too driven to the new. All I hear from Spotify is "Here's new stuff, here's the stuff that came out today, here's the stuff that came out last week." And that's cool, and I like discovering new music, but what's nice about the For You feature, at least for me, is like "Oh my god, I liked this album when I was in college. I liked this album when I was in high school. This album reminded me of the summer of 2006." And there was some discoverable stuff sprinkled in there. So that mix, to me anyway, felt much better and much more interesting than Spotify: "Hear all the new shit. Listen to the new shit. Here's all the new shit." That accelerated, sped-up, gotta have the new thing – the stuff that they're serving here is much older and I think that's enjoyable for me.

KB: All right, Cortney, so what are your final *final* thoughts on Apple Music.

CH: Final final! I don't know, I mean, three-month free trial. Try it, why not.

## Thanks:

I have to start by thanking John Chandler, who gave me a shot at the Rocket when I was a goofy high school kid, and then again at the Portland Tribune in 2004. None of this would have been possible without you giving me those chances, and I probably would have gone to law school. My parents hate you.

Huge thanks also to Bill Werde, who brought me into Billboard and taught me so much about the business. Thanks also to Rob Levine, who mentored me and taught me how to be an editor and a leader. Other Billboard (and ex-Billboard) crew who get love: Lou Hau, Ann Donahue, Laura Leebove, Chuck Eddy, Ed Christman, Jason Lipshutz, Jill Mapes, Antony Bruno, and Glenn Peoples.

Thanks to the Cuepointers, Mike Pizzo and Jonathan Shecter, for giving me free reign.

Kyle Bylin, the best podcast co-host a girl could ask for – you rock. Our Skype conversations will be in the National Archives some day. Thanks also to Bruce Houghton for helping us spread the gospel, and all our guests for chatting with us.

Thanks to the teams at Thinglink, official.fm, Gumroad, Superglued, Soundrop, Muzooka, Revelator, and Buster for being fun to work with.

Marley Degner and Amy Vecchione have known me longer than anyone not related to me and still like me anyway, and for that I am ever grateful.

Sarah Jaffe, Sonia Aneja, Beth Weinstein, Mary Harvey, Julia Khvasechko Garling, Erica Silbiger – thanks for being awesome drinking and/or running buddies.

Jeff Stokvis puts up with far more talk about the music business than any person should have to, and remains patient, steadfast, and wonderful. I love you.

Ozen the dog is the single best canine assistant around, and provides snuggles when I need them.

Thanks and love to Jessica and Brian Orth and Olivia and Hudson, and sorry I foist all those apps on you to test. And the biggest love and thanks of all to Ken and Rosemary Harding, the best parents I could ask for. You encouraged my independence, creativity, and endless questioning nature, and for that I'm forever in your debt.